Praise for *Holy Love*

"A must-read for anyone sent to this earth to love. So, all of us. I wish this book had been given to me when they were handing out condoms in sex ed. Seriously, it's transformation wisdom we all need for fulfilling relationships."

— **Emma Mildon**, bestselling author of
The Soul Searcher's Handbook and *Evolution of Goddess*

"*Holy Love* is a bone fide curriculum for those who aspire to move beyond becoming worthy of love to becoming love itself. The authors deftly explore the multidimensionality of the relationships among Soul, ego, and inner child in both a fluidity of spiritual languaging and a savvy psychological vocabulary. The generous inquiries, journaling exercises, and meditations offer a sophisticated alchemy of transformative experiences. The personal stories wonderfully illuminate the entire process. A gem!"

— **Linda Graham, MFT**, author of *Resilience: Powerful Practices for Bouncing Back from Disappointment, Difficulty, and Even Disaster*

"Whether it's our relationships as best friends and business partners or the relationships we have with our significant others, we are reminded every day how much our spiritual growth happens in relationship. *Holy Love* is meeting the world at the most Divine time. Has there ever been a more potent time to revolutionize the way we love and connect with ourselves and others?"

— **Lindsey Simcik** and **Krista Williams**,
cohosts of the *Almost 30* podcast

"*Holy Love* taps into the deepest truth of all relationships: underneath all the roles, the widest aspect of the relationship is Soul to Soul. This larger perspective, when integrated into relationships, expands the nature of all interactions and uplifts us, our relationships, and our world. Both the tangible and intangible d others as Souls are immeasurabl u get there."

— Annie Burr ig ul

"Love. It's right up there with air, food, and water as one of our most vital ingredients for existence. And yet it is often misunderstood as well as difficult to find and keep. Until now. *Holy Love* is a masterclass on the true meaning of love and provides an expansive curriculum and formula for a deep, Soul-driven, love-filled life. Highly recommended for all students of love."

— **Arielle Ford**, author of *Turn Your Mate into Your Soulmate*

"One of the most important tools for navigating life successfully is the ability to look within and see your part in it. Adam Foley and Elisa Romeo have written a book that truly embodies the feeling of being with them. They are loving, kind, patient, honest, and connected — connected not only to each other but to themselves. This book beautifully guides you through the process of cultivating that skill for yourself through stories, examples, and powerful prompts. Your life is waiting for you to see what Adam and Elisa are showing you in this book. Joy, peace, and growth are waiting on the other side."

— **Danica Patrick**, professional race car driver, author of *Pretty Intense*, and host of the *Pretty Intense Podcast*

"Packed with spiritual wisdom that comes to life through fascinating stories, *Holy Love* does a beautiful job of describing everyday steps for bringing your highest, most loving self to any relationship."

— **Erin Leyba, PhD, LCSW**, author of *Joy Fixes for Weary Parents: 101 Quick, Research-Based Ideas for Overcoming Stress and Building a Life You Love*

"*Holy Love* meets us on the bridge between our hearts. And it provides us with the tools we will need to remain there, deepening together over time. Elisa Romeo and Adam Foley understand something that few humans do: They understand that we are not just here together to keep each other company. We are here together to show each other God. The portal is each other. I can think of no greater teaching."

— **Jeff Brown**, author of *An Uncommon Bond* and *Grounded Spirituality*

"Love is what we crave and also what so many of us fear or never had modeled in healthy ways by our caregivers. *Holy Love* gently and beautifully guides you toward the true connection you deserve. What a wise, honest, kind book."

— **Jennifer Louden**, author of *The Life Organizer*
and *Why Bother?: Discover the Desire for What's Next*

"*Holy Love* helps us break free from unfulfilling scripted expectations and move into a deeper and more fulfilling way of relating. Its helpful exercises guide you to find your truth and share it with your partner. Enjoy it, and live and love better."

— **Gary S. Bobroff**, author and founder of Jungian Online
and JUNG Archademy

"In this beautiful and powerful book, Elisa Romeo and Adam Foley remind us that when we keep our hearts open to each other, we are also opening to the Soul in each other. Through utilizing relationship as the foundation for spiritual growth, they show that love is truly spiritual in nature. With curiosity, profound insight, and humor, this book provides the practical tools and insight to navigate the ups and downs of daily relating with grace, and offers the possibility to emerge knowing a Soulful and fulfilling love."

— **Claire Bidwell Smith**, author of *Anxiety: The Missing Stage of Grief*

"*Holy Love* dispels the myth that the spiritual path must be a solo journey. The world is ready to move on from the pseudo-enlightened alone-on-a-mountaintop model of spirituality. If you want to truly grow, apply your practice to your relationships."

— **Jonas Elrod**, writer/director of *Wake Up* and *In Deep Shift*

"Close, intimate relationship might be said to be the Asclepion healing temple of our time. It is no secret that when we take the risk to allow another to matter to us, we open a portal for our entire unlived life to pour through. Elisa Romeo and Adam Foley offer an alchemical road map and modern way of Soul-tending that uses relationship as the path, shining a warm, compassionate, and insightful light into the mysteries of the heart."

— **Matt Licata, PhD**, author of *A Healing Space:*
Befriending Ourselves in Difficult Times

"*Holy Love* will shift the consciousness that lives in your heart! It is a powerful and inspiring reminder that our relationships are sacred and so precious. Through practical, digestible, and enlightening stories and exercises, Elisa Romeo and Adam Foley show us how to turn intimacy into a fulfilling spiritual practice. If you are looking for real strategies for daily living, but also profound possibilities, this book is for you."

— **Melissa Ambrosini**, podcaster, speaker, and bestselling author of
Mastering Your Mean Girl, Open Wide, and *Comparisonitis*

"This offering from Adam Foley and Elisa Romeo is to me one of the most timely, profound gifts of this new era and one that not only meets our deepest secret desire for fulfillment but holds our hand and walks us to it. When Elisa first told me that she and Adam were writing this book together, I almost cried. More than tears, though, my body is lighting up with a remembrance of how good life can be when we are not so constantly distracted from our Soul, the Soul of our partner, and the Souls of all the people we relate to every day. Mark my words: this book will go down as one of the most thorough, expansive, important books of this new era. Elisa and Adam are a teaching union like no other — no BS, funny, but also in touch with realms that transport us home. I feel so lucky to receive this wisdom from these two, and it will be at the top of my list of gifts to give people I love."

— **Peta Kelly**, author of *Earth Is Hiring, Stop Missing the Point,*
and *Earth to Kids*

HOLY
LOVE

HOLY LOVE

The Essential Guide to Soul-Fulfilling Relationships

ELISA ROMEO, MFT, and ADAM FOLEY

New World Library
Novato, California

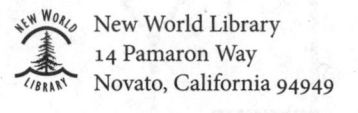 New World Library
14 Pamaron Way
Novato, California 94949

The material in this book is intended for education. No expressed or implied guarantee of the effects of the use of the recommendations can be given or liability taken.

Text design by Tona Pearce Myers

Library of Congress Cataloging-in-Publication data is available.

First printing, February 2022
ISBN 978-1-60868-802-9
Ebook ISBN 978-1-60868-803-6
Printed in Canada on 100% postconsumer-waste recycled paper

 New World Library is proud to be a Gold Certified Environmentally Responsible Publisher. Publisher certification awarded by Green Press Initiative.

10   9   8   7   6   5   4   3   2   1

To our boys:
Non conoscevamo l'amore Divino
finché non abbiamo conosciuto Voi.

Contents

List of Exercises and Meditations..xiii

Introduction..1

Chapter 1: **What Is Holy Love?**...7

Chapter 2: **Holy Lovers Are Mystics**..13

Chapter 3: **The Four Spiritual Relationships**.............................29

Chapter 4: **The Ego-to-Ego Relationship**..................................35

Chapter 5: **The Ego-to-Soul Relationship**.................................53

Chapter 6: **Hearing Soul's Wisdom**..73

Chapter 7: **Healing the Inner Child**...93

Chapter 8: **Tough Love**..103

Chapter 9: **Meet Their Soul**..115

Chapter 10: **Seeing the Soul**..135

Chapter 11: **The Soul-to-Soul Relationship**............................157

Chapter 12: **Soul Sex**..175

Chapter 13: **Soul Communion**..197

Acknowledgments...201

Notes...203

About the Authors..207

List of Exercises
and Meditations

Emotional Reflection Guidelines..47

Emotional Ping-Pong Inquiry..49

Meditation: Feeling Peace...50

Soul Memories Inquiry..67

Meditation: Introduction to the Soul...................................68

Soul Journaling Instructions..87

Soul Journaling Prompts..90

The Feeling Chart...99

Soul Journaling Prompts for the Inner Child.............................100

Inner Child Play Date..101

Inner Child Affirmations...102

Tough Love Inquiry...111

Relationship Check-In Inquiry..112

Their Soul Nature Inquiry...127

The Head versus the Heart...127

Heart Expansion...130

Meditation: Meet Their Soul..131

Seeing the Energy of the Soul..145

Eye Gazing with a Partner..147

Withdrawing Projections..149

Beyond the Label..151
Meditation: Seeing the Soul...152
Silent Togetherness Practice...166
Soul Contracts Inquiry..167
The Four Spiritual Relationships Exercise........................168
Mystic Mad Libs..170
Soul Eulogy..172
Your Pilgrim's Call...186
Red Light, Green Light...188
Mystical Chairs..190
Sex without Touch...192
Soul Sex Guidelines...194

Introduction

You may not realize it, but your whole life has been a crash course. All of your most important memories have been part of a living syllabus. From the first moment you gazed into your mother's eyes, you've been front row in class. That horrible fight with your childhood friend, the crush at summer camp, your first kiss, and the first time "going further" were all part of the curriculum. Your first serious relationship, the horrible breakup, the feeling of being utterly alone, and then ecstatic makeup sex were all assignments. The unexpected shock of betrayal and the conscious decision to forgive were tests. From sitting bedside during the loss of a loved one to witnessing the birth of new life, you've been learning. Delight, joy, trauma, contentment, conflict have all been intensive subjects during your immersion in Love 101.

We can interpret these life moments as random — a constant stream of accidental events — or we can see them as signs of purposeful training. We have all studied at Love University and gone through the beautiful and painful experiences of what works and what doesn't work when it comes to loving another person — and ourselves. Hopefully, most of us have learned a thing or two since our first awkward hand-holding, but few of us knew what true ends we were working toward.

When we were young, we did not choose love; it chose us. At first, a curious glance caught another's, and a small ember ignited the center of our heart. This initial encounter with love felt like nothing short of a spiritual experience. We sensed an inexplicable allure, mystery, and excitement. For a moment when we were in this exalting state, the world was birthed anew. The veil was pulled back, and life suddenly seemed rich and radiant. The burdens of the mundane fell away, replaced by an inhale to a riveting existence. We felt a secret significance, without knowing why. Here stood love — new, unencumbered, pure, and with no manual. Life itself became purposeful, meaningful, and sacred. Before we learned to be cautious in relationships, we let the fire grow wild, generous with its flames.

Then, the majority of us experienced the crushing heartbreak of our first fall from this rapture. The disruptive, cold, hard reality settled in. We all have different stories of our first disappointment in love. Maybe the feelings weren't mutual, or our beloveds chose someone else. Maybe they were defensive, traumatized, or noncommittal. Commonly, after the initial awe, the realization sets in: we've given our heart to a complete and utter stranger. Their love potential has been replaced by the messy reality of their wounded humanity. The character beginning to develop before us in no way matches up to the heavenly inhabitation we initially believed them to be.

No matter what your recollection is of your first fall from love's grace, we've all learned that relationships can come with a whole lot of grief. Over the years, our love manual has become less of a sacred text and more of a tattered survival guide. We've been so wounded by love that many of us have become cynical, believing our natural youthful hubris was misplaced and false. We will not be played as

fools, so we bury the hopeless romantic within, rid ourselves of ide-
alism, and settle for a compromise of the original vision. We label
the few of us still clinging to this image of enchantment "delusional
dreamers." We take what we can get while slowly losing hope that
such an absolute love is even possible.

Shakespeare conveniently killed off Romeo and Juliet before
we could discover if they would have survived the ups and downs
of long-term relationship. Yet we believe his intention was to invite the audience to wonder: Were they just young, foolish, and
naive? Was their love true or merely romantic projection? Would
the flame have died down over time? Or was it everything Romeo
and Juliet believed it to be, a union cut out of the stars — fulfillment incarnated? The story of Romeo and Juliet has endured
through the generations because it speaks to us. Married, single,
gay, straight, polyamorous — we all are suckers for a good love
story. Within even the coldest of hearts exists a spark that, in the
end, wants to be witnessed in love, as love. Despite the layers of
protection we've placed over them, our hearts still silently sing
when the story ends with a kiss. The wounded cynic within argues
that such a love exists only in fairy tales, but the Soul yearns to be
truly seen and, finally, deeply recognized and loved.

All this because we were never shown what love could actually be. The reason our relationships fall short is because we were
never given the map of how to find each other on a Soul level.
For most of us, this elevated form of love was not modeled by our
own families growing up, and we are definitely not given clear
directions in romantic movies. But a part of us always knew, and
knows right now, that the ember burning in our hearts was not
placed there only to be extinguished. This longing yearns for true
union. Part of us knows: we came here to love.

There is a higher love — the communion of Souls. Not to be
confused with the hot, explosive, fizzle-out eruption of projective

love, Soul communion is wholly sustainable. In fact, it is the *most* sustainable type of love, because it is the only form of love that is truly eternal. When you connect with anyone on a Soul level, you connect to the infinite part of yourself, the other, and love, which all exist beyond death. Embodying love is the ultimate spiritual legacy we are here to incarnate.

This love between Souls lives in constant revelation and unfolding. It overtakes us in electrical states of union. It causes deep attraction, a passion that seizes the entirety of our being. In this union we feel rapture at her voice, revelation in his hands, and awe in their embrace. Intimacy begins to feel like worship in bodily form — a love that is a true marriage of two complete selves. Holy Love blends our finite character into our more Divine existence, creating heaven on earth. In Soul communion we no longer love each other; we become love through each other. In this love, as love, we are finally no longer alone. We are seen, we are met, we are loved utterly and completely.

The world opens to us again. We witness miracles and nature illuminated. When we leave our homes, the beat of our heart ripples outward, growing through every encounter with each person we meet. Internal love and external life no longer hide from each other in secret corners but commingle and merge in harmony. We become conduits for a state of love consciousness. Pleasure is not a distant word but a song pulsing throughout the body. We are no longer searching for meaning — we can taste meaning, touch meaning, have sex with meaning.

Love is our spiritual superpower. It has the strength to change our lives, our relationships, and the world. Reacquainting ourselves with the holy and transformational nature of love does take some practice. We need mental clarification coupled with embodied action. The path of consciousness is to know love — to become crystal clear on what it is and *what it isn't*. This book

maps out the grounded information as well as providing meditations, inquiries, and practices to apply it to your life. The path of
Holy Love is a sacred undertaking for those willing to be transformed. Instead of giving or receiving love, we become love itself.

We are about to amplify the dimensions of all of your relationships. Through our unique method of implementing the
Four Spiritual Relationships, we expand your understanding and
tools for communication and true Soul intimacy. As we impart
the skills of Soul conversation and communion, we lay out the
foundation to transform any relationship into a spiritual one. You
elevate your communication skills from mere mental engagement
to deep heart transmission. You become proficient in receiving
Soul's information to navigate practical daily life. This program
can be used whether you are married, in a long-term relationship,
in a short-term relationship, or single. The techniques work in all
relationships: with friends, children, family members, coworkers,
neighbors, acquaintances, and even people you have just met. You
can utilize these techniques if you are in a happy and thriving relationship or if your relationship is in need of work and has little
to no intimacy.

One thing we truly appreciate about these skills is that they
benefit relationships even if the other partner is unaware or un-
willing to do the work. What we have repeatedly noticed is that
the moment one person in the relationship steps into the energy
of their own Soul, a powerful shift is immediately felt by both par-
ties. While it is true that we can never control another person, we
can control the energy we bring to a situation, greatly influencing
the dynamic between us. Ultimately, this method introduces a
complete and total love into all your relationships.

Our hope in writing this book is to help you shift the Soul from
an intellectual concept to enlivened embodiment. The Soul is not
known through rational thought. Holy Love calls on us not only to

think but to feel the deeper intentions behind the symbol of language we share, offering spiritual transmission and transformation. For this purpose, we have capitalized particular words that warrant reverential acknowledgment and that the intellect can see only obliquely, such as *Soul, Divine,* and *God.* Throughout the book we also capitalized *Holy Love* to remind us of the particular and sacred nature of what we are summoning within our lives.

This book is meant to serve you in whatever way best suits you. You may complete all the exercises and meditations chronologically, or you may choose to jump around and focus only on those that particularly call to you. Some may read the book in its entirety and later come back to the exercises, while others may like to complete them as they progress through the reading. Everyone is at a different place in their Soul journey, so there is no one "right" way to be with the content and practices. Do what feels right for you. We offer the exercises and meditations as suggestions, not requirements.

Together, through this book, we will discover the deeper love story behind all the confusion and challenges we face. This book serves as the guide your Soul remembers but has no tongue to speak of yet. It will awaken an intuition you've had all along. Can you hear the whispers of your original desire? Do you remember a love instilled in your bones? Are you ready to come home? If you are prepared to allow all of your relationships to become a portal to the Divine, we invite you closer. Welcome to *Holy Love.*

CHAPTER 1

What Is Holy Love?

Love is a condition so powerful it may be
that which holds the stars in the firmament.

— MAYA ANGELOU

At the risk of being interpreted as solely religious, we have
purposely chosen the term *holy* for our title. A word often
reserved for saints, prophets, and God, *holiness* brings a sense of
reverence, deep presence, and numinous perspective to the concept of daily relating. Whether we identify as religious, spiritual,
or agnostic, most of us can agree that love is our most sacred gift
and birthright, embedded with incredible potential to transform,
heal, and spread grace upon each and every moment it touches.
The phrase *Holy Love* reacquaints us with love's original intent:
a force pulling us together for connection, total acceptance, and
absolution.

People often assume love is supposed to make them happy and
then are shocked to discover that happiness is as complicated as

relationships are. When our expectation of happiness is not met within our relationships, we begin to doubt the nature of love itself. This is because we are culturally fed an *ideal* of love, which carries with it an *ideal* of happiness. When this false notion of happiness is not met, we settle for kind-of love, part-time love, or even in-denial love. These sad options are a result of clinging to an *ideal* of love rather than allowing *real* love in to radically heal our lives. We have forgotten the spiritual nature of our love. We treat love like a drug to take away our pain, seeking an anesthetic for our internalized wounds, fears, and illusions. But in truth, love is a crucible.

A crucible is a trial or test so powerful we are forever transformed for going through it. When we listen to the innermost core of our hearts, love calls us on a journey. Love silently pulls us through the trials and endeavors of our relationships into the potential of a previously untapped union. This journey teaches us about our needs, desires, and, ultimately, ourselves. When we allow ourselves to experience love in its true state, it does not mask our pain but, rather, promptly reveals our conditioned patterns and emotional triggers. The relationship we originally sought for a steady source of solace may suddenly become one of the greatest sources of frustration and challenges. We think we have drifted off course, but in actuality, this is the next destination where love in its wisdom wanted us to land and inevitably find ourselves. Like an oyster transforming a grain of sand into a pearl, love transforms indispensable, unavoidable emotional grist into absolute healing and beauty. Love is not only a feeling; love is a process. When we allow it, love holds us close, then wears us down to surrender into our most fulfilled selves.

We do not need to settle, ignore, or blind ourselves to enter the kingdom of love. Love is by far the most powerful force on the planet. When understood and correctly tapped, love's transformational power is bound to change anyone within range of its transcendent nature. Problems that used to feel insurmountable are radically altered once seen from the vantage point of love. Love brings the sublime to the daily, activating the ability to see the mundane with eternal eyes. Love catapults the monotonous into Divinity, transforming hell on earth into heaven on earth. This book is ultimately about igniting real love in our lives and becoming more of ourselves in the process. Holy Love is just this: love as a tool for embodying truth through relationship so that we ultimately become more of our whole, individuated, authentic selves.

In its etymology, the word *holy* is derived from the concept of wholeness — not unlike our modern concept of holistic health, which includes psychospiritual (emotional/spiritual) well-being as well as physical well-being. More importantly, the word *holy* implies that only in the merging of these two halves, the spiritual and the physical, do we become whole. Holy Love begins when relationship serves as a catalyst to embody Soul. This alchemical process within relationship creates an intimate union unlike any other: a holiness between two Souls.

We recently asked several clients to describe what Holy Love felt like for them. Emily and Jackson were married for six years before they started to treat their relationship as a spiritual practice. In a session Emily described this shift: "There was always a part of me that couldn't see Jackson. I kept making him responsible for my old wounds, even though I knew he wasn't the cause of them. But I couldn't help myself.... Since I've learned to focus in on his Soul, I could cry at any moment, seeing how incredible he is."

Another client, Charlie, shared a similarly potent transformation: "Honestly, I think we both didn't really know each other very well. We were so caught up in our miscommunications, we were missing each other completely.... I kept trying to prove myself to her.... Now, I feel as if I never really have to explain myself again. I am heard, felt, and recognized." And one attendee at our summer retreat described the experience in somatic terms: "When I connect to her Soul, it feels like the sun coming down on me. I am filled with warmth. And she feels powerful, yet gentle. In those moments, I feel wrapped up in joy, I feel completely full of love."

Love as You Are

Holy Love is not about chasing some magical fairy tale of spiritual romance. Holy Love is a result of clearly seeing each other for who you inherently are. We don't need to do anything to *become holy* — we only need to stop the patterns, habits, and mental interpretations that block us from our holiness. In the end, Holy Love forces us to drop egoic agendas, false perceptions, and complex strategies of defensiveness and manipulation in favor of the raw, real, and simple experience of connecting to each other.

To love truly, we must first understand our true nature. Our true identity is our Soul identity; therefore, true love originates on a Soul level. Most of us live just shy of understanding this part of our nature and thus are reduced to sleepwalking as humans and as lovers. Soul love wakes us from our slumber and reveals a vivid new reality. How can we find a Soul mate if we can't see and feel the Soul? How can we connect with someone else on a Soul level if we do not connect with our own Soul personally and intimately? This process transforms the very foundation of our identity, if we allow it.

The distance and disconnection we feel from our own happiness and fulfillment are equal to our lack of ability to love. Bridging the empty space between two people is more profound than most realize. Because love is our spiritual purpose, the more confident we become in our ability to love, the more we become our true selves. Over time, this cosmic line between *the way in which we love* and *who we are* dissolves, until they are one and the same. True love connects us with the innermost part of ourselves. Once we stop underestimating and limiting love, our relationships become a spiritual path to the Soul. In this book, we use love and relationship as a portal to understand and become our most Divine selves. Relationship becomes the worldly arena for incarnating a sacred love in ourselves and others.

We do not need to go externally searching to bring Holy Love to fruition. Rather, the search is internal — it happens as we unearth qualities, abilities, and wisdom that have previously lain dormant. We all have known Holy Love deep in our Souls, but most have yet to see those moments for what they are. Recognizing the presence of Holy Love currently within our everyday lives is the first step to utilizing this spiritual superpower to transform our relationships and change our lives. When we align with a Soul-level love, our relationship shifts from a series of compromises and misunderstandings to a place of nourishment, rejuvenation, and profound truth.

Most of us have known this pure Holy Love, but only briefly. The smile of our child when we pick them up from school can fill our hearts with ineffable good. Our first kiss may flood us with total elation. The touch of our wife's hand on our back in a time of hardship may give us strength we did not know we had. The embrace of our lover can melt us into a state of complete gratitude. Sharing time with a friend over tea can elicit immeasurable meaning. Glimpses of Holy Love permeate our lives — all hinting at a more Soulful version of self and a better life. Holy Love elicits the best and truest part of us.

It may seem heretical to claim holiness in such ordinary human emotions. Yet once we begin to identify these moments when we are connected to love, we notice a timeless and spiritual quality. Love is complex and multilayered, but in its unhindered nature, love takes the form of pure admiration and contentment with existence itself. What is love if not holy?

Within these moments of intensified love, we return home to an inherent happiness and inexplicable contentment. For a moment we are whole; for a moment we are holy. These are the memories that allow us to cultivate discernment on our journey toward total fulfillment. These moments help us identify what feels authentic, true, and Soulful. In this recognition, we already bring to consciousness a truth known only through experience. Because love lifts us to the Divine, love is inherently spiritual. Love not only links us to the eternal but is our true legacy of how we lived while on this planet.

Unconditional love is eternal love, existing even beyond death. Even in the healthiest of relationships, most people assign conditions to love, conditions buried away in their subconscious. Few of us have truly known what it is to feel totally and completely loved, thereby missing the healing potential of love. We block love's full embrace, not always due to the fault of our partners, but often because we unconsciously hide and edit ourselves. We ultimately cannot be truly seen if we are hiding.

The issue is not that we are missing Holy Love in our lives; it is that we have fallen into an emotional fatigue of sorts. Unresolved trauma, pain, complexes, and grief estrange us from complete acceptance of ourselves and our loved ones. Most of us currently wear blinders, allowing us to glimpse only a portion of love's rays. The good news is that Holy Love is like the sun. The sun does not stop shining, even if hidden by clouds. Like a stormy sky, our pain blocks our capacity to believe and remember the sun is still shining behind it all. Maybe the storm has gone on for so long, we have forgotten the sun even exists. But with spiritual practice, we can position our Soul like a magnifying glass, find the light, and concentrate love into a fiery beam for holy consummation and utter joy.

CHAPTER 2

Holy Lovers Are Mystics

*Longing takes us back to God, takes the lover back into the arms
of the Beloved. This is the ancient path of the mystic, of those who are
destined to make the journey to the further shores of love.*

— LLEWELLYN VAUGHAN-LEE

We began our immersion in Love 101 at birth. When we came into this world love was new, unchallenged by our expectations, disappointments, and self-made beliefs. Then, as we grew older, something changed. When we reached out for this perfect love, it faded away as the reality of this world settled in. We came here with a blueprint etched into our hearts, a map within our cells, an intuitive knowing of a perfect love that called to us but did not always match up to the life given to us. We learned that love comes with all the complicated conditions of being human. We could almost touch and hold this perfect love, but only partially, for brief moments. We knew a craving in our Soul that seemed to find no satiation.

We all have that hunger in us, yet how we respond to it widely

varies. The way we cope with this deep longing determines who
we are. There are several different ways to relate to the calling for
a higher love. We can deny, manage, or be transformed by our
search for the beloved. This core human desire creates three types
of people: the pragmatist, the rationalist, and the mystic.

We are taught the ways of the pragmatist early in life. We are
trained to focus our attention on the external world. We are told
our hunger will go away when we have social and material success. We are told to feed our craving for love with things. But no
prize can fill the hole in our heart.

The pragmatist blames their unhappiness on circumstance.
They create a long list of "if onlys," telling themselves if life were
different, then they would be fed and satiated. If only they were
paid more at their job, their Soul would be fed. If only their parents had raised them better, their Soul would be fed. If only their
spouse would change, their Soul would be fed. If only they had
been dealt a different hand, their Soul would be fed. They are left
reaching for the proverbial carrot that is always out of reach.

Some never evolve past the pragmatist in life, but most of us
experience the rude awakening of disappointment. We come to
realize that even when we get what we want out of life, circumstances change, and we are still left with our spiritual hunger. This
disappointment creates the second type of coping: the rationalist
mindset.

The rationalist attempts to subdue their hunger pains through
self-proclaimed disillusionment. They tell themselves that their
expectations of love were simply too great. Perhaps they were
naive to believe in a life that could ever satisfy them. They accept
starvation as part of being human. They hunker down into their
circumstance as if in a well-fortified castle and look down at those
who still believe that life can be more than this.

The rationalist, believing they have found the truth according to all known evidence, doubles down on their conclusion. They become fundamentalists of reason. They disown the spiritual hunger in themselves and project it onto others. As their suppressed hunger tries to suppress the hunger in the people around them, they cynically claim that any intuitive behavior or thought is delusional. They associate mysticism with an avoidance of reality, but it is the rationalist who is in avoidance of reality. For the rationalist, what is "real" is only what is quantifiable and empirically provable. Reducing life to what is measurable not only is based on false assumptions but also brings with it tragic conclusions.

The rationalist may have proven their hunger for perfect love is false, but they have also disproven the existence of a perfect love at all. They have used their power of mental will to stop themselves from perceiving their hunger, but also from perceiving Holy Love. They trap themselves in a cold, meaningless world. Many people remain rationalist their entire lives.

But even the rationalist is not completely successful in subduing their hunger. They can stop themselves from believing in their hunger, but they cannot stop themselves from *feeling* it. Those who are in touch with their feelings and aware of this hunger become the mystics.

As we consciously accept the inherent longing for Holy Love in our lives, we naturally become mystics. In fact, Holy Lovers *are* mystics. A mystic is someone who craves direct intimacy with the mysteries of the universe. Mystics are not satisfied with stories about love; they want to experience love personally. A mystic is someone who prioritizes the unseen, felt inner world over the external physical world. The mystic senses more, sees more, feels more, and, ultimately, wants more. In relationship, a mystic sees through surface appearances while also feeling the inherent potential of the connection. This potential is not delusional or foolish but arises from faith in the as yet unmanifest spiritual intention of the meeting. Similar to a healer holding the vision of a healthy leg beneath a very apparent physical wound, the mystic senses an underlying deeper potential than is present in most average surface relationships. Because of this orientation, the mystic also desires to be *seen and met* on a deeper level than in most average surface-level relationships. The mystic is not satisfied with acquaintance-level conversation or the dopamine hits that come from approval or social status. They have an inherent integrity and require honesty, meaning, reverence, and true connection in relationship. A mystic does not settle for a mere companion to keep them company, but desires to meet another on a Soul level.

Mystics are oriented to seek meaning, resulting in a deep and often complex relationship with their feelings. Regardless of their IQ (intelligence quotient), mystics inherently have a high EQ (emotional quotient) and SQ (spiritual quotient). This gives them a high sensitivity and awareness of the energy (tone or atmosphere) of any room they walk into. In personal relationships, they may even relate more to their partners' subconscious energetic intentions than to their literal words or actions. Because of their heightened sensitivity, mystics often feel alienated and isolated from the majority of the rest of the world, which is often more material-world focused, straightforward, and simple.

At times, high EQ and SQ can feel like an overwhelming handicap, but they can be incredible tools if understood correctly. Having them is akin to owning an incredibly sensitive and powerful jet engine but never having been taught how to use it properly. It could create a huge amount of damage if used incorrectly, but once understood and mastered, it becomes a potent vehicle with which to navigate new heights of emotional and spiritual dimensions within relationship.

With this great potential before us, why is it that heartbreak is much more common than heart union? The problem is that most mystics don't know they are mystics. In an attempt to fit in, many mystics compartmentalize or minimize their deep inner longing for a spiritual and Holy Love. Yet, once they understand their inherent mystical nature, the old inner script of self-sabotage naturally reveals itself to actually be one of self-empowerment. They recognize and accept that each feeling, impulse, and intuition for deeper connection, which used to feel like a hindrance, is in fact imbued with great spiritual purpose and direction. They discover that every relationship issue has a spiritual solution, once they teach themselves to notice and listen to these inner signs. Mystics love differently than the other types. When the mystic gets to know what love *really* is, they begin to unravel the mysteries of the universe.

The mystic knows this: they were never innately broken, created to crave what they cannot have. They simple mistook love to be of this world. The problem was never that the food of the Soul did not exist — it was that they were seeking to fulfill a mystical longing through earthly means. The mystics are in contact with what is *most* real. They know that those who exclusively value the visible world as reality are truly the out-of-touch ones. The mystic does not avoid their internal hunger but trusts and listens to it, understanding it as a sacred Morse code. This language of the Divine holds messages that they can feel and translate through humility, surrender, and an open heart. They allow their hunger for perfect love to consume them, guide them, and ultimately heal them.

Once we stop suppressing our hunger and accept it, we realize it is not hunger at all, but homesickness. We long for the home of love — the experience of oneness with Divine love. We long to be utterly consumed by love. We want love to fill us entirely, pump through our veins, beat in our hearts, and radiate from us. We want to become love itself.

In this world, we find the comfort of home with the people

we love. It is true that home is where the holy heart is. Of course, our literal childhood homes, where we were raised, may not have provided the home we desired in our hearts. But with the Four Spiritual Relationships, we can create home with the people we choose, our Soul family. We can finally and truly feed our Souls when we consciously create home on earth with one another.

. Home is a quality, not a place. Home is where we seek refuge after life slams us down. We are home when we know unconditional acceptance, forgiveness, and gratitude. We come home when we are recognized for who we really are. Home is when one person sees another and says, "Yes, you, too, are a miracle." Home is spiritual absolution.

The paradox is, when we let go of trying to *get* love (like the pragmatist) or *disprove* it (like the rationalist), we can finally *receive* love as it is. All relationships are, in fact, fundamentally spiritual. A spiritual relationship is not something one acquires. Our relationships become spiritual when we behold the Soul in one another. We stop trying to *get* something from our partners to feed the endless internal hunger. Instead, we recognize the same hunger exists within them. In this recognition, we see we are the same. We realize love *is* our hunger. Love *is* our desire to seek the holy in one another. Love *is* our longing for the meeting of Souls. Love *is* our craving for the real and the eternal. The desire to love is our calling to love. Once we stop trying to *get* love from one another and finally *receive* love together, *through one another*, we know Holy Love.

You may wonder how we, individually and as a couple, have been initiated into this experience of Holy Love. Throughout this book, we share our own personal stories of waking up to our true identity as mystics and how we have come to this work of the Soul — or, more aptly, how our Souls came to work us. The following is the story of how Adam became conscious of his own deep longing for and awareness of Holy Love. Sometimes, life teaches through the extremes of violence and death, making obvious where love has been absent. Wherever there is violence, there is an inability to see the Soul of the other. The value of these tough life experiences is that, through extreme contrast, we are intimately introduced to our deepest true and holy nature.

Adam Speaks

When I was fifteen, I left the United States for a yearlong exchange program in India. I did not know why I was called to India in particular, but I did know I wanted to escape the emotionally cold atmosphere that pervaded my childhood home. The exchange program offered the opportunity to finally discover if other families had what was missing from my own life. For the first three months of my journey, I was in culture shock, living with a host family that hardly spoke a word of English in the poverty-stricken town of Malegaon. My host father, Rajiv, would say Malegaon was famous for its large vegetable market, but to most it was known for its large — and economically suppressed — Muslim population. As soon as I arrived, I was warned not to walk down the streets, for animosity and violent acts between the Hindus and Muslims were not uncommon.

I was enrolled in the local school. Unfamiliar with Hindi, I wasn't learning much from a class taught entirely in that language, but I tried my best. One day, as my mind zoned out in a wishful attempt to subconsciously soak in the language, a boy came running up to the window. He slammed on the glass, turning every head. "Bomb!" he screamed, terror in his eyes. "Bomb!" I don't know if he yelled in English for my benefit, but that was the end of the information I was going to get. The class went into immediate panicked commotion. The students sprinted out the door. There seemed to be no evacuation plan but to run.

The school was empty within minutes. I found myself standing alone in the schoolyard without a clue what to do next. Before I had any time to think or seek safety, Rajiv came tearing down the dirt road on his motorcycle, a cloud of dust gathering behind him. He skidded up alongside me. "ON!" he screamed. I knew there was no point in asking him to explain, through his broken English, what was going on, so I surrendered to his guidance.

Within moments we approached a large crowd on the verge of a riot. Rajiv plummeted the motorcycle into the heart of the throng. We made our way through with pure force, knocking over a few unfortunate bystanders. On the other side of the confused mob, I saw a police barricade blocking the only bridge into town. I realized that these were families anxious to see if their loved ones were safe. Rajiv headed our motorcycle toward a familiar face along the police lineup. Rajiv was personal friends with the police chief — they had grown up together. After they exchanged a few words, his friend motioned for the other cadets to let us through, to the utter dismay of the increasingly tense horde.

As we crossed the bridge and headed toward home, it felt like we were crossing over to hell itself. Bodies slouched against the crumbling railings; dirty blood dripped off the sidewalk. Rajiv continued at full speed, apparently more focused on keeping me safe than on checking if these ravaged people were still alive. I screamed at him to stop, but he either couldn't understand me or chose not to. As we entered the town, I heard only two sounds: the roar of our motorbike and the distinct point when a scream turns to weeping.

When we approached the house, I could see the center of the blast. I made out a distant pile of bodies, some still moving. Rajiv pulled up to the front door. "GET IN!" he yelled. I protested; my instinct was to run to those people and see if I could help. Rajiv jumped off the bike and grabbed me by the arm. He forcefully threw me through the threshold. I began to beg, "Let me help!" Without a word, he removed a padlock from the inside of the door, slammed the door behind him, and locked it from the outside. He was locking me in his home to keep me out of harm's way. I pounded on the door, but I already could hear his motorbike's engine revving up, and he was gone.

The house had roof access but no escape to the street. The rest of the afternoon I spent trapped as I helplessly watched the nightmare unfold from the rooftop. My host mother used the roof to dry her clothes, and it had been my favorite spot, but now it felt like my personal prison. The ambulances arrived but were inefficient on the narrow dirt roads. Soon, volunteer pickup trucks joined them.

The following twelve hours were a blur. The emergency relief continued into the night. I can't remember how many victims I saw taken away. There were so many wounded they had to be carried away by the truckload. One I remember in perfect detail to this day: a woman thrashing in the bed of one of the pickups — her legs gone, replaced by loosely wrapped bandages. I could recognize in the pit of my stomach that her screams were not from pain but from heartbreak. It was then I saw she was cradling the small shape of a child wrapped in cloth.

The next morning the streets were completely empty except for an occasional lost wanderer in a state of grief. The news was coming in now. This had been a coordinated attack targeted at a Muslim mosque on the Muslim holiday of Mid-Sha'ban. A large group was leaving the mosque when three bombs had gone off. More than 40 people were killed, 125 severely injured.

Around midmorning, my host family and I were shaken out of our emotional fog by a knock on our door. Rajiv stood to go inspect our visitors. When he returned, he was trailed by an entire news crew. Cameras and lights poured into our small living room.

They wanted to interview me. I was the only American to ever live in Malegaon and one of the closest witnesses to the event. Rajiv had already agreed on my behalf, and the crew was setting up. In my shock I didn't know how to say no, though I desperately wanted to.

When the camera clicked on, I emotionally poured out my heart. If there was a chance the interview could support a message of peace after this travesty, I wanted to use it. I begged for understanding and compassion, reminding the audience that despite different beliefs systems, we are all mothers, fathers, and children.

After the crew left, I assumed this would be the last of the media arriving on my doorstep; I was wrong. The story went viral because I was a rare American living with an Indian family only a block from the explosion. The news teams grew larger and the coverage more in-depth. I was filmed walking around town with a Muslim friend of mine, Yousef, to show the potential for peace during a highly tense time. The news teams encouraged me to wear traditional Indian clothes to display my affection toward Indian culture. And they continued to invade almost every aspect of my life with my host family, following me as I cooked with my mother, played with my cousins, and visited the blast site itself. Eventually, I told Rajiv that I would not do another story until I had my own time to process the experience, but by then it was too late.

I received a call from the United Nations. They informed me I was the next target for an upcoming terrorist attack. My peaceful stance had unwittingly made me a symbol within a long-term political drama I barely understood. Upset extremists were focused on my whereabouts, so the UN urged me to evacuate the country as soon as possible. I began receiving emails from family and friends at home, demanding I return to the States. But I could not.

I had come to India seeking answers, but now I was left with more questions. After witnessing intense suffering and death, I

was catapulted into an existential crisis. My nightmares revealed
the cold panic of survivor's guilt. Previously, I had been privi-
leged, idealistic, entitled, but also hopeful. Before the bomb blast
I considered myself an atheist, but I still believed in a world of
meaning. I sensed there must be some purpose behind the events
of a life. Now, that belief had been violently ripped away from me.
Something had changed in me forever, and I knew I couldn't go
home until I had resolved the haunting new existential dilemma
inside my chest.

I abandoned the exchange program, left my school, cut all
ties to the friends I had made, and took off on my own across
India like a homeless ghost. I was just sixteen, but never had the
mechanics of life and death been so abrasive to me. I hadn't previously believed in God, the Soul, or an afterlife, but now I craved
something supernatural. Either my existential wanderings would
come to some mystical conclusion, or I would seek the emptiness
of death in order to be released from the pain. Either way, I was
determined to end this suffering.

After traveling solo for a month, avoiding contact with
friends or family, the isolation began to feed my death wish. I finally sought out companionship using my exchange program di-
rectory. I needed someone familiar to me but not too intimate. I
found this in a seventeen-year-old German student who invited
me to visit. Andreas lived a day's trip away from where I was,
and with no better place to be, I caught a train and arrived early
the next morning. He gathered all the local exchange residents
to meet me at an underground dive bar. It was only 9 a.m. — a
potential warning sign. In my excitement to speak English I over-
looked it.

The social scene quickly disintegrated into a drunken frenzy
as my new acquaintances ordered one pitcher of beer after another. I soberly played pool in the corner; getting belligerent was
not what I needed at the moment. Andreas had brought his blonde

American girlfriend. She hadn't spoken a word all morning except for a few childish whispers to him. After another pitcher, he began to make out with her. In India, public displays of affection are not only extremely offensive but also illegal.

The barkeep, a short and muscular man, approached Andreas and tensely asked them to stop. Andreas shrugged his shoulders, like some high school cliché, then stood up and walked, with his girlfriend in tow, directly into the women's restroom. To walk into a women's restroom in India crosses so many cultural gender taboos, it's equivalent to spitting in someone's face — more particularly, in the face of an already fuming bartender.

I watched, completely mortified, as the furious barkeep flexed his fists, stormed into a back room, and returned with a crew of taller, more menacing-looking men. They waited in silence until Andreas showed his face again. "GET OUT!" the barkeep shouted. "F*CK YOU!" Andreas shouted back. Then, all of the exchange students joined in: "Yeah, go f*ck yourself!!"

In a moment of hopeful naivete, I stepped in. "Hey, everybody! Let's all calm down…" Everyone continued yelling. "Let's go, it's not worth it," I coaxed, trying to herd the students out the door. Andreas had one foot out the door when he grabbed the waiter closest to him and threw him onto a table. Then Andreas leaped out of the doorway, like an evil Peter Pan, and ran off. He left me alone, with five angry full-grown men behind me.

The first swing was to the side of my head and sent me staggering sideways. Before I felt the pain, my knees began to buckle. I grasped onto a table as blackness seeped into my vision. I looked up and saw daylight pouring down a cement staircase into the entry a few feet away; I remember thinking it looked like the gates of heaven. I was so close to escaping.

When the light came back I was surprised to see I was still standing, but I couldn't move my arms; two men had them pinned down behind me. Three others stood in front of me, drunk with rage. The first punch hit my ribs, knocking the wind out of me. The second hit my stomach; nausea and pain surged through my body. The third went straight into my left eye; my head swung back. Then everything slowed down; I felt like the room had been submersed in molasses. My mind teetered as it made sense of my situation. *They could beat me to death; I might die.*

I considered it — surrendering to death. In the confronting clarity of this moment I was faced with the conscious choice that had been unconsciously following me for months. After the terrorist attack I had been submerged in survivor's guilt. The intense poverty and illness, the incredible contrast between a spiritual homeland and unsettling death had been haunting me. *Where was the meaning of life or God when the streets were filled with scattered bodies? Could I actually participate and choose to live in this horribly painful and unjust world?*

During the beating, I had not fought back. My instincts were at battle. I didn't know if I should resist or submit. Since the explosion, I still didn't know what I wanted more: life or death? If life was purposeless, why prolong it?

Another swing hit my side; I sheepishly looked around the room.

The dirty cement walls, spilled beer, and hanging lamps glowing low — how strange that this bar was the last place I might see, my gateway to either a homecoming in the afterlife or a deep, dark sleep from which I would never awaken. I looked into the eyes of the men in front of me. All I saw was pure rage. They were so angry, so misunderstood. Why could they not see me? They didn't even know me, yet I could feel hatred pulsing through their eyes into me. So bizarre, this not-seeing-one-another that could actually end in my death. Had they always been this angry? I imagined them as children, hearts open, pure, and playful.

I could suddenly see much deeper. Behind their eyes the layers peeled back: at first sorrow, then fear, then loneliness, then helplessness. *In fact*, I realized as I slouched toward the floor, *they feel more helpless than I.*

The next thought zapped like an electric shock down my now-feeble body. *They don't know themselves! They cannot see beyond what they understand themselves to be.*

Another fist landed in the center of my chest. I was entering an altered state of pain and passivity. Now, on the brink of nonexistence, deep acceptance of this moment surfaced within me. My senses heightened as the liquid of love slowly filled me. I felt I was awake to the present moment for the first time in my life. Compassion greater than anything I had ever known — for myself, but also for these men — overcame me. And finally, after months of suffering, I felt clarity.

I was immediately aware of two separate stories within myself. I felt a source of compassion encompassing me that had a running narrative of love, and I also sensed the density of my own human consciousness with its potential for the story of separation. I recognized as well this story of separation in the men before me. Although they were experiencing relief from their helplessness, they had not been introduced to the more powerful story of the unity that existed in the space between us. They had unleashed their pent-up anger into an addictive fury and ecstatic release. Although intimidating, the hatred felt flimsy. They had projected the false power of anger upon me; I just happened to be its sacrificial victim. They believed that overpowering me would take away a sense of powerlessness they had grown used to living with. However, I knew two things: not only was it a false and temporary power, but this moment was offering me an opportunity to discover real power.

A wave of newfound energy hit me, and my body heightened

with animalistic instinct. Life was more than enough to fight for. I lifted my feet off the floor; the two men holding me up leaned forward to counteract the weight. Then with all my strength I kicked my two feet off the ground, tipping the men backward, just enough to temporarily loosen their grip. I wrangled my arms free and launched my shoulder into one of the men in front of me. He toppled over a chair. I swung at the man directly blocking the door. My fist hit his cheekbone, and he stood stunned for a moment. I lunged for the door and to my surprise started climbing the staircase.

I came up on the sunny sidewalk. The city was bustling, vendors on the streets, rickshaws honking; life looked jarringly normal. I jogged a few blocks, until I saw no one was following me. I walked on, noticing all the noises and people around me. The sun was dazzling. Everything looked different — alive, clear, humming with meaning.

To this day I still don't know how I accomplished what I did, except that a pure will to live or maybe a pure will to love overtook me.

My journey in India continued for another six months, but now with more purpose. I sought out gurus, sadhus, mystics, and many different spiritual teachers. I had seen a glimpse of something more, and I couldn't shake it. On the edge of death, I was taken to a place of *seeing beyond*. In this heightened state, it was crystal clear exactly where the limitations of egoic (or separation) consciousness block us from love. An incredible compassion was startled awake in me in that very moment. The blows to my head had unlocked a powerful opening in my heart. I loved those Souls I saw suffering that day. I recognized their suffering. Just as the sparks of stars are masked by daylight, but in the space of darkness their heavenly eternal allure is revealed, I was shown a glimpse of Divine beauty within the contrast of pure hate.

After this experience, I saw everyone differently. Not only could I feel and identify the divide we all experience between our idea of self and our true love nature, but I could also feel the pain this divide creates within all of us. For most people that pain remains unconscious, but it nevertheless remains. The way we choose to deal with the pain determines who we become. Holy Love offers us a way to use our longing to come home to the truth of who we have always been behind all illusions.

CHAPTER 3

The Four
Spiritual Relationships

Mysticism is only a transcendent form of common sense.

— G. K. CHESTERTON

We used to believe the world was flat. Sailors feared exploring the unknown. They dreaded the tides that might pull
their ships off the face of the planet into nonexistence. In the third
century BCE, the early astronomer Eratosthenes proved these
mythic sea tales wrong with the astounding calculation that our
home was truly a sphere. Yet for hundreds of years society denied
his discovery and chose to live in an illusionary flat world. The
sixteenth-century explorer Ferdinand Magellan is quoted as having observed, "The church says the world is flat, but I know it is
round, for I have seen the shadow on the moon." He and his crew
were the first to circumnavigate the world, shifting our known
paradigm forever.

Similarly, most of our relationships are flat. We impose one-dimensional limits on our potential to love. Many people will never tap their love potential because they mentally block their own understanding of their true identity. As we begin to connect to Soul (the eternal love self), however, we discover there is more to ourselves and what is possible in love than we ever could have imagined. We all have an ego, and we all have a Soul. So we are truly multidimensional beings, which means our relationships are also multidimensional. "Multidimensionality" may sound like a complicated, slightly science fiction–esque concept, but it simply means that we communicate in ways both conscious and unconscious, both physical and energetic. As with the law of gravity, we don't have to believe in it to be affected by it.

To be multidimensional means we exist on more than one plane. We are all multidimensional, even if we don't know that about ourselves yet. We all send and receive energetic signals — even the individual who identifies as existing purely on the material plane or the mental plane. Sometimes, through meditation, a spiritual awakening, or an out-of-body near-death experience, a person glimpses a broader part of themselves that they may not have known previously. They begin to feel and know themselves as an energetic presence, made up of more than the constant stream of thoughts produced by the monkey mind.

The concept of our multidimensionality may be hard to wrap the mind around, but we must remember the fate of our early astronomer Eratosthenes's discovery. For those who lean toward heady analytical thinking, multidimensionality can be confusing, but within the realm of tangible experience, as in Magellan's circumnavigation of the globe, we live through and accept broader realities. We want to invite you to keep an open mind while conducting your own exploration of love through this book. To enter multidimensional consciousness, we first must expand how we perceive love and relationship. Then the real reward begins in the application and integration of Holy Love into our own lives.

Humans are walking paradoxes. We can be self-destructive, hyperemotional, and divided between conflicting impulses. It often appears our minds are programmed for short-term, conditional affection while our hearts are designed for everlasting and unconditional love. All too often we fall into automatic behavior within relationship, without our own or our partner's best interests at heart. With no better alternative, we settle for repeating the same relationship mistakes over and over. The differences between us and our partner multiply, wounds deepen, and our Souls are left feeling utterly and completely alone.

The solution to this cycle of misunderstanding is to become conscious of ourselves as more than the ego personality and to engage in relationship from a broader vantage point. Instead of a singular relationship, we actually have four relationships to be mindful of, which is why we call this relational work the Four Spiritual Relationships (see figure 1). First, we have the relationship of our own ego to our partner's ego, which is the external ego-to-ego relationship. Second, we have our own personal and internal relationship between our own ego and our Soul, the ego-to-Soul relationship. (Though we will be exploring this relationship in chapter 5, we recommend Elisa's book *Meet Your Soul* for further reading and a deep dive into that relationship.) The third relationship is our ego's relationship to our partner's Soul, the ego-to-their-Soul relationship. And fourth, we have the Soul-to-Soul relationship, which contains the Soul lessons and contracts that hold and alchemize the entire partnership. Do not worry if this sounds confusing for now. We will be covering all of these relationships in depth throughout the book.

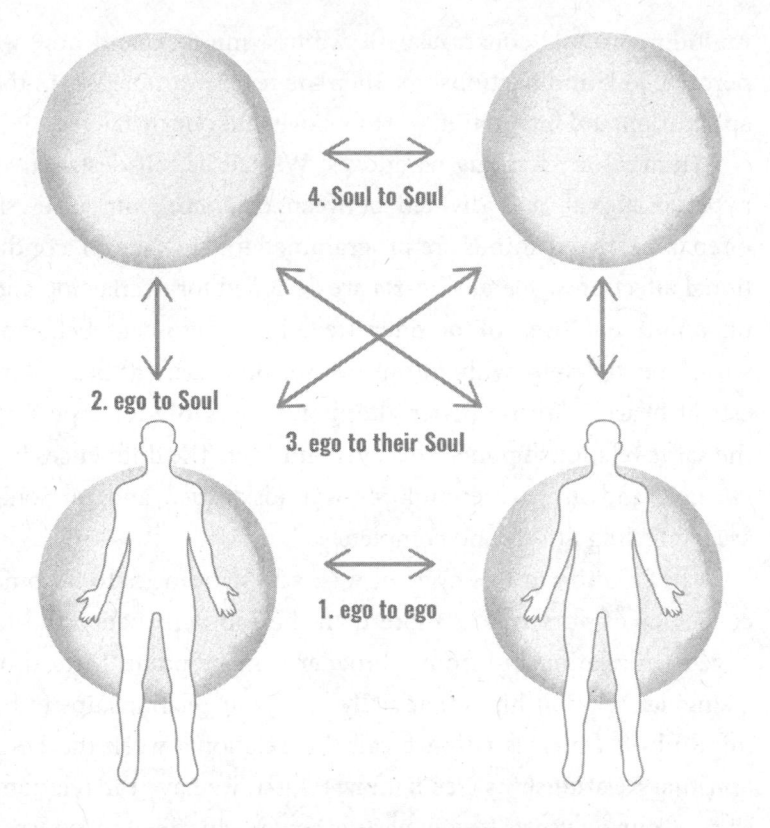

Figure 1. The Four Spiritual Relationships

Confusion in relationships most commonly arises when we attempt to resolve conflicts while we are still in a conflicted state. When a relationship conflict seems to have no resolution, it is only because we have not yet gained our spiritual sight. The Four Spiritual Relationships are an astonishingly useful tool. With them as our guide, we become aware of the source of others' pain, nonreactive to trauma projected upon us, and wise in our words and actions. This drastically increases the chances of survival and the healing potential for any relationship. We move from the old pattern of "Your hurt feelings hurt my feelings" (which creates an endless destructive spiral) to actually listening to the higher directives of love. The Four Spiritual Relationships help us identify and discern what part of ourselves we are acting (or reacting) from and how to become clear on what part of others we want to invoke.

With this system of navigation, we enter into a whole new playing field. We learn to raise our consciousness to the level of love. As we introduce the Four Spiritual Relationships into our lives, our stresses, misunderstandings, and differences will be exposed for their limitations and healed.

Holy Love does not take sides; it does not need to win or gain approval. With Holy Love, our view of our partner transforms from a source of stress to a sanctuary of ease. With the four relationships as our blueprint, we trade conflict for forgiveness, expectations for acceptance, and points of friction for transformation. Following the guidance of Soul, we navigate our partner's false beliefs, pain responses, and trauma to meet on a heart level while discovering the unconditional love that resides in us all.

CHAPTER 4

The Ego-to-Ego Relationship

You fell in love with my flowers but not my roots,
so when autumn arrived you didn't know what to do.

— ANONYMOUS

*E*go often means different things to different people. It is a word that is used in many different ways. Sometimes it implies arrogance: "That one has quite an ego!" In some religions and spiritual communities, ego is considered inherently negative, and our sole task is supposed to be to transcend, dissolve, or annihilate its dominion over our lives. This sentiment is conveyed by the popular T-shirts and bumper stickers that remind us, "Your ego is not your amigo." Traditionally, in psychological terms, the ego is considered to be an important part of our identity — a necessary element of the psyche that facilitates reality testing, healthy self-esteem, and the ability to set boundaries. Yet even within the myriad of therapeutic modalities there are varying interpretations of what ego is and is not.

In *Holy Love*, for all intents and purposes, we define *ego* as "who you think you are." The ego is our sense of personal identity, heavily influenced by our culture, our belief system, and our interpretation of the world. Icebergs appear large and majestic but display only a portion of their entire structure above the surface of the sea. The remaining mass is submerged beneath the water (see figure 2). Similarly, the ego may appear to be the sum total of a person, both to the individual and to others, but it is only a fraction of our nature. Upon deeper inspection, we discover that the unconscious, the emotional/energetic body, and the Soul are also essential, yet often hidden, parts that make up the greater whole.

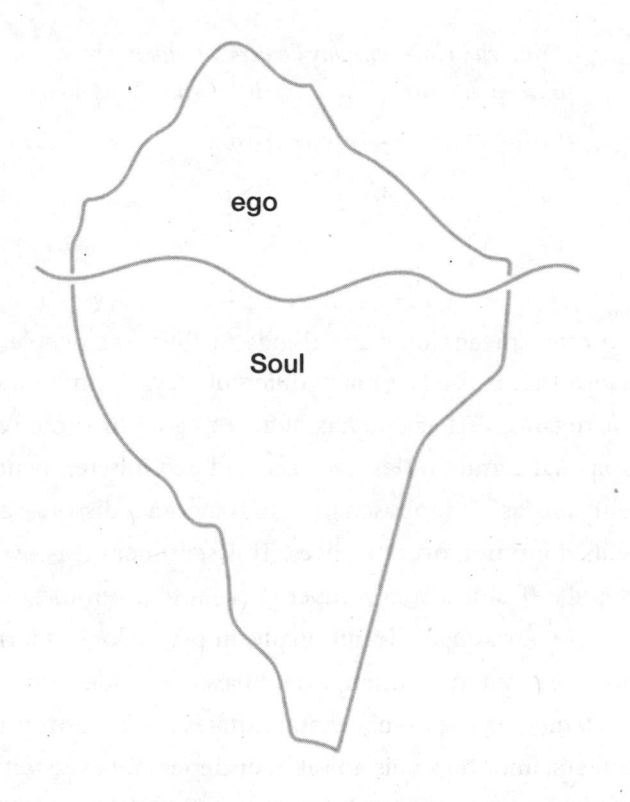

Figure 2. Like an iceberg, we are made up of the visible ego and the greater mass of the often hidden Soul.

In our day-to-day lives, we usually remain unaware of these hidden parts of ourselves. This is why the ego is often surprised when symptoms from these inner characters rise to the surface. For example, in a yoga class, a young woman may burst into tears during Pigeon Pose, unaware that she unconsciously held painful memories of abandonment in her thighs. Or the jealous lover may scream out profanities, only later to apologize sheepishly: "That's not me. I'm really not like that. I never talk like that." Which begs the question, just who then was speaking?

For Soulful intimacy, a healthy functioning ego is essential. Like the liver, the ego serves as a filtration system. Ego integrates spiritual experience into thoughts and words and translates wisdom into action. But ego needs to be seen as just that, the heaven and earth intermediary. Ego often remains trapped in rationality, convincing us that our human condition is material and finite. Our intuition, on the other hand, senses the greater potential that life holds, including new dimensions of untapped love. It is by balancing rational thought with spiritual intuition that ego incarnates the eternal love that will serve us in spiritual intimacy. Ego by itself can be limited and even destructive. Ego when oriented to love has the potential to be the hands for the Soul in the world.

We Are Holy and Human

Our decision to name our mystery school and podcast *Holy & Human* was very purposeful. We know that to have deeply fulfilling relationships, we must be conscious of both the human (egoic) and the holy (Soul) levels within our relationships. When we meet Soul to Soul it is a holy exchange; when we meet ego to ego it is a human exchange; while ego-to-Soul relationships are an interweaving of the two (see figure 3).

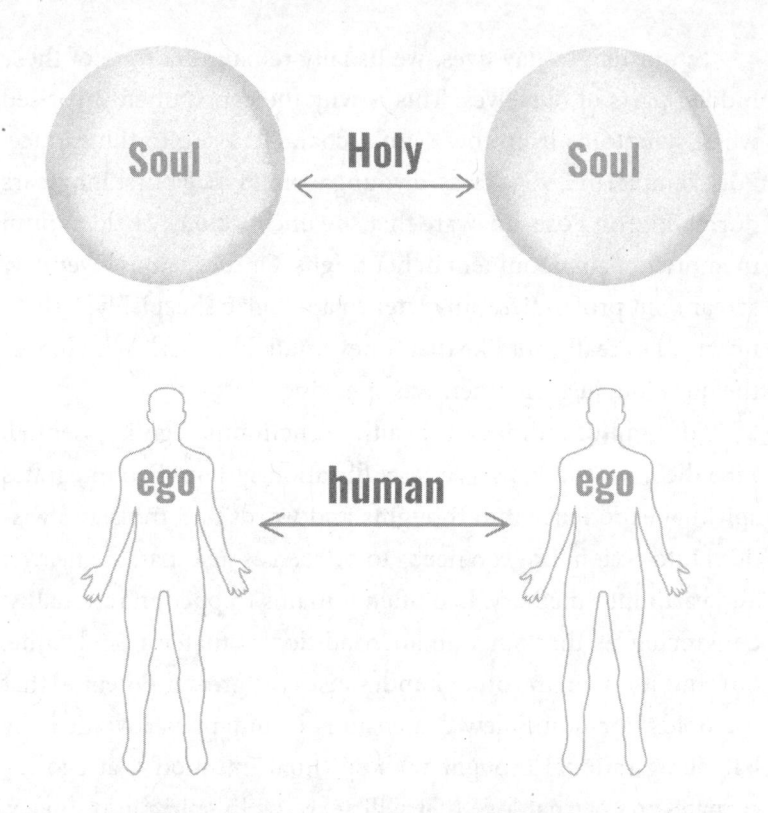

Figure 3. Holy versus human relationships

If we neglect the holy level of relating, we may show up in the human realm — doing our part of the housework, communicating our needs while acknowledging our partner's, and making life goals together — but the relationship may lack deeper connection and intimacy. Conversely, if we negate the human realm and rely solely on the spiritual connection, we may be at risk of minimizing the (very human) importance of showing up consistently for others, being accountable for our own behavior, and owning our personal responsibility for our inner development. To honor the holy in each other, we must first honor the human in each other. We have seen far too many examples where the strong "spiritual connection" with another has been used to excuse an unhealthy human level of functioning, without an ability to set healthy ego boundaries.

Examples of a Healthy Ego

It can be tricky to identify healthy ego functioning. Many people believe that the more confident someone is, the greater the self-esteem they carry. This may be true of confidence, but hubris is something else altogether. Ego identity is our personal narrative of who we believe ourselves to be, which includes how we describe ourselves. Ironically, when someone is boastful or has what we would call a huge ego, it is not a sign of healthy self-esteem but actually indicative of a weak ego. An overcompensating attitude of "I am always the best" is often a defense to avoid being vulnerable and navigating deeper feelings.

A healthy ego gives us a generally positive interpretation of ourselves along with an assumption that we are worthy of healthy relationships. This inherent self-esteem allows us to have the confidence to identify what we like. We know we want Indian food for dinner and can communicate that desire to our partner. A healthy ego has the confidence to try new experiences and push us a bit out of our comfort zone. Healthy egoic functioning can set longer-term goals, like training for an upcoming marathon, saving money for a house, or planning a dream African safari trip together.

A healthy ego is capable of critical thinking. We examine the rules we have been taught by our families of origin and use discernment to live by a social code we deem to be valuable and fair. A healthily functioning ego can also adapt to stress, is resilient, and is capable of regulating painful emotions. This creates an ability to flow with what is happening in the moment and a general flexibility in life.

In egoically healthy relationships, partners have a mutual

respect for each other's unique desires, dislikes, goals, and values (see figure 4). The self-esteem of each partner is strong enough that it does not crumble in the face of a dissenting opinion or viewpoint. Even if we disagree with our partner or friend, we can reflectively listen to them and make them feel heard and respected. In these healthy relationships, each individual is capable of managing their own disappointments and other feelings, leaving them free to hold space for the authentic emotional process of the other person without passive aggression, judgment, or manipulation.

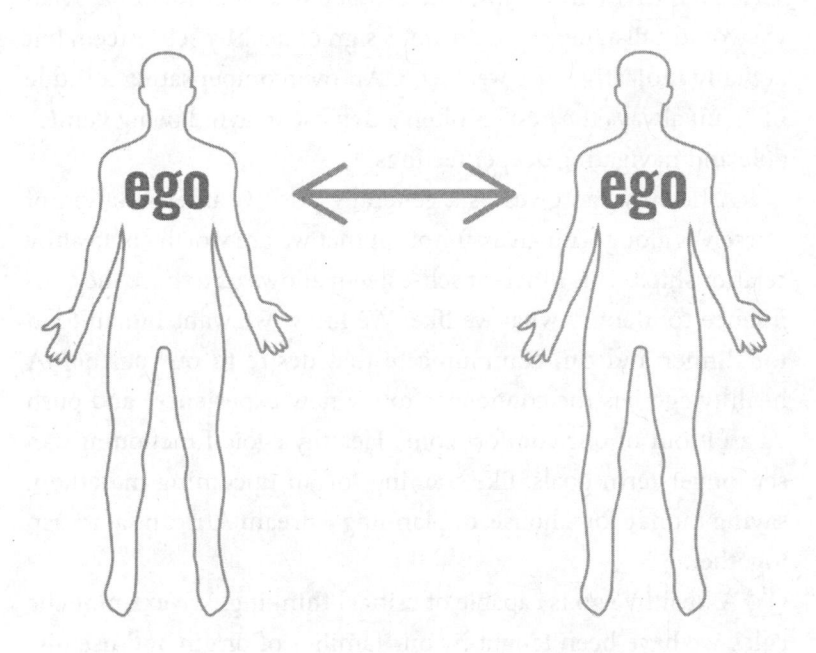

Figure 4. The ego-to-ego relationship

Egos with a healthy inner narrative are capable of setting boundaries. They know they can love the other person while also loving themselves. They have identified their own needs and have the strength to communicate and stand up for what they require

to be healthy. Besides setting the boundary, they have the forti-
tude to hold it if it is tested, knowing that they have set it out of
love and not as a personal attack.

While healthy egos can tolerate some emotional discomfort,
individuals with weak egos become frozen, avoidant, stubborn, ·
rigid, or even rageful if their sense of ego identity is questioned.
Lacking the healthy self-esteem and resiliency that allow them to
handle triggering situations, they become defensive and cannot
stay openhearted. For someone with low ego strength, healthy
communication can be very challenging. Even when they receive
a critique that is given lovingly, they may become flooded with
emotional overwhelm, unable to find the healthy inner resources
to cope with the moment. They are like a tree that is so rigid and
dry, it topples over in the slightest windstorm. If it were more flex-
ible and rooted, it could handle the storm.

For individuals with weak egos, this lack of flexibility becomes self-perpetuating. They cling to unrealistic expectations
of life or of their partners to solve their inner turmoil and take
away their feelings of inadequacy. Instead of holding a mature
perspective of life and others, they rely on the people, places, and
things that will continually align with their limited view of themselves and the world. When that limited view is challenged, they
respond with even more rigidity and anger, remaining stuck in
old patterns and behaviors. Sticking to what feels comfortable and
avoiding what does not, they become emotionally stunted, avoiding the experiences that would actually help them develop their
maturity, adaptability, and ego strength.

At the end of this chapter we have included several exercises
to help you build healthy ego strength, which will benefit you as
an individual as well as your relationships. Much of this book
will also help readers develop a healthy ego, in particular chapter 6 ("Hearing Soul's Wisdom"), chapter 7 ("Healing the Inner

Child"), and chapter 8 ("Tough Love"). It is a gift to our loved ones to make our ego relating as healthy as possible. The benefits are that we live with strong self-esteem, take ownership of our inner world, live with clear boundaries, and engage in healthy communication.

The ego is essential, and we cannot bypass the value it brings to our lives and our relationships, but it is also only one version of ourselves. Now that we understand how a healthy ego is crucial for healthy relating, let's talk about the limitations of identifying and relating *solely* from the ego.

The Limitations of the Ego

Unfortunately, we often abandon our Soul nature to play a role, and our ego totally identifies as the personality or the persona. *Persona* comes from Latin and originally referred to an actor's mask. We are in the middle of a modern-day egocentric epidemic caused by an overidentification with our roles, resulting in spiritual amnesia. Cut off from Soul, we become hypnotized by our ego's memorized lines. After playing our part for so long, we stop seeing ourselves outside of the flimsy character with which we identify. It becomes impossible to decipher where our true opinions, feelings, and nature reside.

The problem with an egocentric identity is that it narrows our experience of ourselves and of the world. The ego is a genius at throwing us off the scent of being. We become stubbornly attached to what we think we want without checking in with our intuitive feelings. We become susceptible to the notion of keeping up with the Joneses and lose connection to the deeper currents of the true self, which is where real happiness and fulfillment lie. Our appearance, our age, our job, our home, and our social calendar sometimes seem the only ways in which we understand and value ourselves or others. Ego dominance convinces us that these material characteristics are essentials on the checklist for finding a well-suited mate — causing us to potentially miss a Soul-delivered partner standing right in front of us.

Most of us spend the majority of our days orbiting our loved ones. We circle around the periphery of the other's true nature, but rarely touch down to their Soul. An entire lifetime can be spent alongside someone without ever seeing into the depths of their being. Like the adult son sitting beside his father's deathbed, now that they are out of time, they become truly present, staring into each other's eyes to really *see* each other for the first time. In a painful irony, only now do they cherish the relationship that in life was seldom valued. Their first real moments together are also their last.

Some relationships are sought out to serve all of ego's requirements — approval, comfort, company, and physical gratification. Unfortunately, we live in a culture where our concept of love values egoic acceptance as the indicator of a successful relationship, with little understanding of Soul connection. Our most popular dating websites utilize questionnaires to generate relationship matches based on beliefs, interests, and personality types, with only egoic compatibility as the end goal. While there is nothing inherently wrong with this approach, it has its limits — it does not account for Soul connection. Then, when the app-generated connections do not fulfill our deeper longings, we wonder what went wrong.

Ego builds the theater of relationship to fill the endless need of an appreciative audience. We are not implying that attraction or desired personality traits in a partner are not Soulfully sanctioned, but most relationships struggle to break through the bind of ego as the default identity. We will never be smarter than our own lies. If we live behind the mask of persona, delivering what we think the audience wants, when we are finally loved, we do not

truly believe it. When we are performing, love never feels legiti-
mate.

If we don't have enough Soulful connection in our lives, we
feel depressed, apathetic, and unlovable. We struggle to reconcile
a deeper, unconscious part of ourselves with the fractured experience of the thoughts and words with which we identify. We stare
into the mirror, and something doesn't make sense, but we can't
put our finger on what's wrong. This type of disconnect is impossible to rationally pinpoint and mentally think our way out of. The
surface appearance of our life does not speak of a deeper truth we
feel.

Relationships that focus only on satisfying egoic desires often
look picturesque on the outside. Picture-perfect bodies, homes,
and cars satisfy the ego, but internally, these relationships are
starved of real fulfillment. In Soul-focused relationships, we feel
that our partners are irreplaceable, whereas in ego-focused relationships, partners are often mere placeholders for desires. Porn
addiction, jealousy, fear of being replaced, and affairs are the common shrapnel of limited ego-to-ego relationships. Soul-focused
relationships deepen with time, while ego-identified relationships
grow more neurotic with time. The most common hallmark of
neurosis is to manically seek pleasure, distraction, or entertain-
ment, mistaking it for true happiness.

Although the ego has many useful skills, cultivating Soulful
relationships is not one of them. Ego dominance keeps us stuck in
unconscious patterns, making unwise decisions in relationships.
When we continually choose unhealthy relationships, accidentally sabotage the relationships we want, or end up in profoundly
unfulfilling marriages, we know we are making choices from pure
ego. We make choices based on *what we think we want* rather than
what we truly need. Ego may be very successful in managing our
external presentation and the tasks at hand, but it is not skilled

at navigating our internal reality. Ego will never be a successful source of wisdom to navigate love.

Elisa recently worked with a young man in his late twenties who was just awakening to his energetic nature. He had gone on a date the day prior, with what he described as a beautiful and sexy woman who had a career as a model. He was physically attracted to her, but when they began to become intimate, he felt something "turn off" inside of him. On an egoic level, this woman had all the physical and personality attributes he had been actively seeking, but his Soul was now beginning to dominate his ability to engage with her and connect sexually. He was frustrated because he didn't know "what was wrong" with him.

In actuality, nothing was wrong — in fact, something was right. In this case, his own energy was giving him intuitive information about the fit of their energetic Soul connection, which was beyond his current egoic understanding. His energy was seeking a type of experience that was more intimate, Soulful, and conscious in nature than this exchange could offer. This was not a problem to fix but, rather, earnest spiritual information and guidance. In this case, this young man's egoic notion of *what he thought he wanted* (which was mostly programmed by society and heightened for him because of her esteemed modeling career) was fighting his actual energetic experience.

Simply by identifying the nature of the ego, we begin to break its dominating tendencies and loosen its grip on habitual patterns. We start to recognize its old tricks, which immediately clarifies the distance between the old egoic identity and the impulses of the Soul. Right away we become conscious of the dichotomy between the voices in the head and the impulses of the heart. Just by understanding the ego, we have paved the path for meeting the Soul.

Authentic relationships have the potential to crack through

the hardened mask of persona. We evaluate or appraise another person, not solely by physical features, social standing, or personality traits, but by a deeper presence within them. With spiritual tools and perception, we learn, in relationship, to love the eternal within the mold of identity and to become loyal stewards of Soul. This is when relationship becomes something more than two connected people; it becomes a journey toward true being. This is what true love seeks. If we can endure that transformation, an eternal Love is waiting for us.

Ultimately, this book is about catalyzing relationship to transform the ego into a channel for the Soul. When we come to realize that many of the ego's gimmicks and facades were built out of cultural programming and fear, we can finally heal and release these old, unconscious patterns. We leave the circus tent filled with funhouse mirrors and return to a deeper heart reality. As we leave warped illusions behind, we come to the shocking realization that our essence was created in perfection and we are meant to love and be loved.

We hope you take away from this chapter that the ego is necessary. Healthy egoic functioning serves all of our relationships. Yet ego without relationship to a deeper part of ourselves leads us offtrack and limits Soul connection. When humbled and in alignment with deep intuition, ego is a useful servant to help us become our true selves. As we said earlier, in order to have healthy relationships, we need to do the required inner work so the egoic level of relationship is in impeccable integrity and functioning smoothly. Without dismissing or attempting to annihilate the ego, we simply hold space for the ego and see it for what it is. We understand the ego is only a fraction of our identity. It may need love and reflection, but it may not always be in alignment with our true Soul self.

For healthy ego-to-ego relating, we first need to master

strong interpersonal communication skills in order to reflect our partner's human experience with compassion and empathy. The following exercises help others feel heard and understood, building the trust needed to do the deeper Soul work that the next chapters move us through.

EMOTIONAL REFLECTION GUIDELINES

Reflective listening is a powerful communication technique that involves two steps. First, we seek to understand each other by paying attention to each other's words, tone, and body language. Then, we verbally offer our understanding of the other's point of view to confirm that they have been understood correctly.

Often, during disagreements, it is challenging to reflect what the other person is saying back to them. But when people feel misunderstood, conflicts quickly escalate. We can lower the emotional volatility of arguments through good reflective listening skills. Remember, acknowledging another's point of view is not the same as agreeing with or condoning behavior; it simply shows that you understand. Conflict is a great opportunity to build further intimacy.

1. **Start with an attitude of respect and compassion for each other.** Keep in mind that acknowledging your partner's reality does not invalidate yours. Even if emotions run hot, we can hold space for differing experiences and interpretations. Two opposing things can both be true.

2. **Practice active listening.** Let your partner know you understand what they are trying to say. Use statements reflecting back what you heard, such as, "What I heard you say was _____. Is this correct?" If they do not feel your interpretation is accurate, keep trying until they

confirm you have grasped it. This is a crucial first step before introducing an opposing opinion. Remember, reflection does not mean agreement.

3. **Use "I" statements.** Once you have accurately reflected your partner's experience and feelings, you may share your own. Turn your focus on what you are feeling or experiencing, rather than blaming or judging the other person. A good template to follow is: "When you _____ [here describe the situation or action as fact, without your interpretation], I feel _____ [feeling]." Here are some examples of how to use and not use this template:

- "When you were late to the dinner, I felt upset." This clearly states the fact ("you were late to the dinner") and how you felt in response ("I felt upset").

- "When you prioritized your time over mine, I felt upset." Stating that your partner prioritized their time over yours is an interpretation, not a statement of fact.

    Another template you can use is: "When you _____, I interpreted that as _____." For example:

- "When you were late to the dinner, I interpreted that as being forgotten." Here the focus is on the speaker's experience.

- "When you were late to the dinner, I interpreted that as your habit of selfishness and self-sabotage." This statement categorizes or diagnoses the partner's behavior.

4. **Identify the difference between the content of an argument and the emotional process.** It is easy to confuse the issue of a conflict with the interwoven emotions. To prevent this, practice self-inquiry: "Am I upset about this specific situation, or is this situation activating

something else I am upset about?" Or engage in inquiry to your partner: "How are you feeling right now? Is there anything else going on you want to talk about?"

5. **Ask your partner if they are seeking comfort or if they are open to solutions.** So many arguments occur when one party is attempting to fix a problem but the other person just needs to vent and receive emotional support, free of solutions. A great way to avoid this is to get in the habit of checking in and asking what your partner needs: "Do you want me just to listen, or do you want my help in solving this problem?"

EMOTIONAL PING-PONG INQUIRY

When relationship discussions get heated, it is common to enter into an emotional ego-to-ego ping-pong game. We like to call this game Your Trauma Hurt My Feelings. It begins when one frustrated partner, acting from a place of wounds and trauma, blames the other for their pain. The energy from the tone, intensity, and content of the exchange triggers the second person, activating *their* wounds and trauma. In self-defense, they lash back, eliciting even more pain and hurt from the initial partner. The cycle repeats, and we have now entered into the ongoing ping-pong game of blaming and reactivity.

The effect of this back-and-forth is similar to pouring gasoline on a fire. We have several ways to avoid this dynamic, and throughout the book we will offer solutions. For now, know that connecting to the energy of your Soul is the strongest way to raise your perspective above defensive reactivity while also still feeling your feelings and doing the necessary human work of being accountable and accepting responsibility.

To begin to gain awareness of the emotional ping-pong dynamic, let's inquire where and why this is most likely to show up in your own life. You may journal with these questions or meditate on them.

1. Ask yourself: What are some memories of times I have found myself to be short-tempered, frustrated, or feeling unheard in a relationship?
2. Choose one instance and answer these questions:

    - In this situation, how did I communicate that to my friend/partner?
    - If I spoke, what did I say?
    - How did they respond?
    - Was there a better (more compassionate, clear, or patient) way I could have communicated?
    - What was I feeling deep underneath that I didn't sense was understood, received, or accepted?
    - What did I want or wish for them to say?
    - Was there something I could have given to myself in that moment — for example, more compassion or patience — that would have calmed my own emotions and altered the experience?
    - Was there a self-affirmation or hopeful phrase I could have reminded myself of in that moment?

MEDITATION: FEELING PEACE

An audio version of this meditation is available for free online at holyandhuman.com/holylove.

Challenging issues in relationships often manifest when our lives are busy and stressful. Taking the time to meditate can radically change the atmosphere of our intimacy. The following meditation is designed to reset the nervous system from a reactive state into one of receiving and giving love.

Find a peaceful place where you will not be disturbed or interrupted. You do not have to sit in any particular meditation
pose. Just take a moment to find a position that is comfortable for you, either sitting or lying down.

We will begin by turning our focus toward our breath. Turn
your attention toward the sensation of breathing. Without
controlling or changing the flow of your breath, see if you can
simply feel the air coming in through your nose or mouth,
down into your lungs and stomach, and back out again.
Spend a few moments becoming aware of this flow.

Now, imagine that with every inward breath, you are breathing
in relaxation. And with your outward breath, you are releasing all the fears, anxiety, and stress from your body. On the
inward breath, imagine the air itself is a peaceful and calming
substance, soaking into your entire body. And on the outward
breath, your worries are being squeezed out of you, as if you
were wringing water out of a wet towel. Take a few moments
with these images. See if you can deepen the amount of relaxation you receive with each breath.

Next, we will imagine we have released all of our stress. It is
OK if there is still some residual stress; this will dissipate as we
continue. Imagine you are soaked with relaxation and pleasure.
As if you are entering the deepest and most peaceful sleep, the
tension in your body is melting away. Imagine that every single
muscle, blood cell, and atom in your body is being soaked and
bathed in relaxation. It is as if you are wrapped in comfort, sink-
ing into one of the most restful states you have ever known.

Now, I want you to pick a color to represent love. It can be any
color, and this color can change if you like, but pick a color

that feels to you like compassion, love, happiness, and peace. Allow this color to enter your heart and spread throughout your chest. Now imagine it soaking down your arms, all the way into your fingertips. This color will also travel downward, throughout your torso, hips, upper thighs, calves, all the way down to your toes. Now imagine it washing over your neck, face, and head. Feel this color throughout you as the energy of love, acceptance, and absolute peace.

Allow yourself to sink deeper into your relaxation. Bring your attention to your breath once again, and allow every breath, inward and outward, to guide you deeper and deeper into peace. Imagine your breath like waves gently lapping the shore; the sound brings you even greater peace and tranquility.

Now, take a mental scan of your entire body, from the top of your head to the tips of your toes. Notice how every part of your body feels. Remember these sensations and know you have created a state of relaxation you can potentially enter at any time. Make the intention that the next time you feel overwhelmed, you will remember and call upon this potential within you.

We will close the meditation by repeating this mantra three times while taking three more deep breaths.

I feel peace. I am peace.
I feel peace. I am peace.
I feel peace. I am peace.

When you are ready, open your eyes.

CHAPTER 5

The Ego-to-Soul Relationship

Before you find your soul mate, you must first discover your Soul.
— CHARLES F. GLASSMAN

We often think of relationship as something we have only with others, but we also have a myriad of inner relationships with different parts of ourselves. The ego-to-Soul relationship is one of these internal relationships. It is an incredibly powerful spiritual relationship. In this sacred meeting, the ego part of us, who we think we are, is introduced to our more vast and higher self, the Soul. Through the ego-to-Soul relationship we learn how to align our smaller self, as ego, with our individuated purpose and inherent wisdom from our Soul (see figure 5). And, as in any relationship, intimacy grows with time and cultivation. The more we invest in this relationship, the more our ego will learn to trust and recognize our Soul's wisdom.

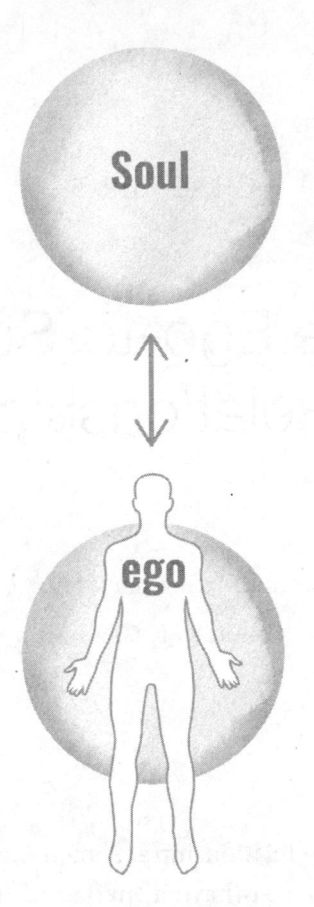

Figure 5. The ego-to-Soul relationship

From the Bible to the Qur'an, from the Torah to the Bhaga-
vad Gita, practically every religion teaches us of the Soul. We can
find the concept of Soul with the Greek Gods of the Old World,
the ancient Gods of Egypt, the mystical Gods of India, and the
monotheistic God of Judaism, Christianity, and Islam. Regardless of cultural differences, physical location, or the continual
evolution of consciousness over time, Soul continues to make
an appearance. Throughout these traditions, the Soul is consistently described as an eternal version of self. This Soul self exists
beyond our understanding of the human personality but is not

without individuality. The enduring phenomenon of Soul around the world proves that, despite our varying belief systems or allegiances to different Gods, most of us intuitively recognize we have an internal, and eternal, spiritual self that exists beyond our human confines. Humans are gifted with self-awareness and consciousness: merely by being human, we have an inherent sense that we are more than merely human.

In common idiom, the word *soul* is used to describe deeply felt emotions or a quality of authenticity. But the Soul is so much more than that. The Soul is our all-loving and all-knowing eternal higher self. Like the blueprint of the fully formed oak tree that exists within the acorn, the Soul calls us to continually evolve into our fully formed and highest expression of our spiritual destiny. The Soul holds our individuated and unique form of love, perfectly tailored to our specific life situations and lessons. Soul is vastly wise but also incredibly practical.

When we connect to the Soul, we gain the necessary inner strength and sovereignty to create intimate and authentic connection with another. But most importantly, we locate the part of ourselves that has always known how to love unconditionally. This source of love becomes our essential guide for all the work that follows.

God and Soul

Though the concept of Soul can serve as a bridge between spiritual belief systems, the term *God* is one that often still separates us. Because it can mean very different things to different people, the word becomes the source of great miscommunication. It is often highly triggering, evoking particular belief systems, provoking hostility, and even reactivating historical trauma between individuals or groups of people.

Our clients come from diverse spiritual backgrounds. Some

are strongly religious; others prefer to identify as spiritual without creed; others identify as atheistic or agnostic; and many prefer no label at all. Working directly with the Soul requires no prescribed dogma, ideology, or strict rules to live by. This is because, no matter what one believes in or which God one prays to, Soul work is about discovering spiritual truth and love *internally*. Ultimately, our highest goal is not to give our students or readers the answers to all of life's questions, but instead to empower them with the intuitive skills of perception so that they experience the big answers personally and for themselves.

In this book, when we use the term *God* we are referencing the unconditional love behind and within all creation, the love that animates everything. We use it interchangeably to mean the energy of love, which strives to unify, transform, evolve, and heal us individually and collectively. The Soul is the individual Divine expression that comes from how God wants to know and experience itself through your life.

If God is the ocean, then Souls are like raindrops. The ocean and raindrops are made out of the same thing, water. When water evaporates, condenses, and then rains down from the sky, the raindrops appear to be separate from the ocean, existing away from it. God (or love) is within each and every Soul, yet Souls are, like raindrops, separate and individual. Souls are individuated droplets of God. We come from love and go back to love, but the Soul's journey is uniquely ours. When we get to know our own Soul, the true nature of our raindrop, we are also getting to know the ocean of love from which it originates. Soul, by its nature, serves as our personal connection to Divine eternal wisdom.

Soul Is Mystery

As long as the concept of Soul has endured, so has our endless debate over Soul's factual existence. Most of us have speculated over questions in our head: Is the Soul real? What truly is the Soul? Do I really have a Soul? Does everyone have a Soul? What purpose does the Soul serve? Many have tried to answer these questions through psychological analysis, the scientific method, or by combing through religious texts. Though all of these methods may provide clues hinting toward the existence of Soul, they cannot prove the Soul's existence. This is because the part of us that wants, or desperately needs, proof of the Soul is the very part of us that is blocking us from Soul's truth: our mind.

In an overly ambitious society, we are motivated by conquest and understanding. We want to understand how the unknown works. We want to know what the stars are made of as much as we want to comprehend the intricacies of another's psyche. But the Soul can never be known as long as we approach spiritual inquiry solely through the mind. For the purposes of this book, we approach Soul using a new, intuitive method. We no longer make a mental decision regarding whether we *believe* the Soul exists. Rather, we reawaken the intuitive awareness that already *knows*, *experiences*, and *remembers* the Soul as real.

The ego wants to feel secure by bringing light to our unknown aspects, but the Soul's truth lies in its cloaked and mysterious beauty. As Joseph Campbell wrote in *The Hero's Journey*, "Life is not a problem to be solved but a mystery to be lived." Soul helps us move away from trying to analyze the spiritual mysteries of our lives and allows us to live in sync within the mystery that is the miracle of life.

That provocative feeling that you are more than this is true. Soul lives within our preverbal state, shining through the cracks of our mind. We can feel Soul's existence in glimpses, sometimes in a dream, through instinct, or in a moment of grace. We often experience it in nature: as we gaze upon a vast starry night or feel the magic behind a luminous sunrise, we feel the meaning inherent in the universe and the sense of a bigger play in which we have a small, but crucial, role.

Whether we know it or not, Soul affects every moment of our lives. Soul is an invisible force, interwoven in our being, nearly impossible to quantify but hosting the seat of all meaning in our lives. Soul is the feeling of purpose beating in our chest. Soul is the spark of our true nature, an eternal guide, and a source of unconditional love. Soul is the fountain of life force pouring from our hearts. Soul breaks through conditioned patterns, appearing as our highest and sainted self in moments of uncanny grace, generosity, and forgiveness. We will never fully understand the Soul, but we can feel the Soul, speak with the Soul, and have a relationship with our own Soul and the Souls of our loved ones. Our ability to hear and connect to Soul determines the most important drive in our nature: whether we wake up feeling alive with passion for life, willing to love and be loved, ready to inhabit our most confident and fulfilled sense of self.

The Soul speaks as a whisper in the back of our consciousness, a voice so close and familiar it may have become forgotten background noise. In college, Adam and his roommates could only afford to rent a house neighboring a high-traffic freeway. At first the endless noise of cars was almost unbearable, but within months he hardly noticed it. In fact, when he went home for the holidays, the quiet absence of the freeway noise felt jarring. The Soul, similarly, exists as a constant stream of self. Soul is a quality running through all of our thoughts, emotions, and impulses, yet most of us have slowly tuned this awareness out over the years.

We are not to be blamed for the unconscious desensitization of the Soul; rather, it's the fault of a culture that encourages mentally dominated living. Like any muscle, our connection to our Soul, when unused and unappreciated, grows weak. With training, practice, and patience, however, we can reacquaint ourselves with our inner strength and Soul's power.

Retuning our minds to turn inward and listen to Soul's steady stream of love is a process, but one that is well worth the work. We no longer feel like motherless children wandering through life, attempting to make the right choices. We are left feeling confident in our own existence. We feel whole. We become one with qualities of joy and grounded belonging. We come to trust ourselves in profound and miraculous ways. We no longer compare, judge, and undermine ourselves but instead relax into our being. When we open to unconditional love, radical healing is instantaneous, as our hearts become reacquainted with the unwavering eternal hum behind and within everything. The only work ahead is not to attempt to solve the riddle of whether or not Soul exists, but just to slow down, listen, and feel. To meet the Soul, we simply open our doors of perception to its subtle language.

Soul Speaks through Intuition

People talk about intuition like it's magic or something reserved for the few, yet we all have access to it. We simply need to reacquaint ourselves with it. Soul is often called the still, small voice for a reason — it is quite common for the noise of the world to drown it out. Intuition speaks to us through the internal details: a pull on the back of our mind, aha light bulb moments, or a soft knowing in our heart. In fact, we already know our Soul, but for most, it is only in fleeting doses that are far too easily dismissed. Being connected to Soul does not make life pain free, but it does immensely reduce the amount of suffering. When we feel confident in the inner spiritual meaning of our lives and the purpose behind the struggles we endure, suffering quickly goes from meaningless to meaningful.

In our relationships it is easy to fall into a mission-driven model of picking our partners apart to figure out what makes them tick underneath the hood. Especially during a rough patch, we can become more critical and complicated in our thinking in an attempt to identify what is wrong — when sometimes getting the answer may be as easy as listening to our intuition.

Intuitive wisdom is often reminiscent of the Greek myth of Cassandra. Cassandra, born the princess of Troy, had the gift of prophecy, but she carried a curse that prevented the townspeople from believing her visions. Most famed for her prediction of the fall of Troy, Cassandra was accurate in her intuition but forever denied validity by society. We ourselves are culturally influenced to disbelieve our intuition, finding ourselves in a similar tortured limbo. Our Souls constantly speak to us, while our minds work to negate our truth. Like Cassandra, we struggle for intuitive legitimacy, but the doubting townspeople have moved into our own minds.

Meet Your Soul's Personality

Philosophers tend to seek out an archetypal and conceptual understanding of Soul. But our search is fruitless if we do not seek and discover the individual Soul. Like a fingerprint, each Soul is unique, and the intricacies and differences are as vast as an entire universe. We must locate the individual disposition of the Soul to know the personality of our essence. Only when we seek the individuality of each Soul will we be successful in entering into Holy Love territory. Getting to know the singular exquisiteness of a Soul is what gives us clarity on whom we love and what our Soul values on the deepest level. This is perfectly captured in the words of John Keats:

> Call the world, if you please, "the Vale of Soul Making."
> Then you will find out the use of the world.... There may
> be intelligences or sparks of the divinity in millions —
> but they are not souls till they acquire identities, till each

one is personally itself.... How then are souls to be made? How then are these sparks which are God to have identity given them — so as ever to possess a bliss peculiar to each one's individual existence. How, but in the medium of a world like this?

If we focus our attention on getting to know the Soul, we will find the Soul is a specific entity in itself. Soul feels, thinks, and has opinions, which are often counter to the ego's. When we begin to connect with our Soul, we will find not only a wellspring of unconditional love but an inner animated character.

Each Soul has its own area of genius, which is our individual path to enter into the Divine. The genius of Soul can vary widely: it might look like a sharp and astute comedic talent, a poetic ability to articulate a feeling, a patient and wise way to connect with children, a natural ability to work with animals, a mastery of learning and communicating through different languages, or an uncanny talent to express emotion through the body as a dancer. When we follow our natural desires, we hone the gifts the Divine wants to celebrate through us. This self is chock-full of stunning individuality. What you love is your path to God, and this is why the Divine appears in the open space where you and your genius meet.

One client, during their first encounter with their Soul, exclaimed, "I feel like my Soul wants to paint! What!? I've never painted in my life." Another described meeting her Soul as being like an endless river of love flowing through her chest. She told us, "My Soul is love, but it is also fierce. I've told myself I should not be so bold in my relationship. But my Soul is extremely confident in what she wants." A single male client once confided in us that he hadn't been on a successful date for five years. After getting to know his Soul's personality, he decided for the next date he would much rather play minigolf than sit down at one of his usual go-to restaurants. This last date blossomed into a significant relation-ship, where he felt much more comfortable to let go and reveal himself. As we get to know the Soul, we experience the miracle of becoming the Divine character we were born to be.

Because we lack intuitive awareness in the modern era, our deeper Soul personalities are rarely recognized by others and even by ourselves. Most of us have been culturally trained to act a certain way or carry incongruent beliefs about the self. Only rarely is our persona shaped into a mirror image of our Soul's personality. Shades of the Soul will always shine through in our idiosyncrasies, but we may need some guidance or reflection to reach full Soul embodiment.

As we reacquaint ourselves with this inner personality, at first it may feel foreign yet familiar at the same time. As we strengthen our Soul communication, slowly the true personality unfolds. Ini-tially our Soul may feel like a stranger, but over time we remember Soul as a truth we have always felt. With consistent spiritual prac-tice, we embody this new yet recognizable personality of Divinity.

Soul Is Not Known, Soul Is Experienced

Soul is known only through direct experience. To know the Soul, we need to meet the Soul. We need to have an alive, personal, and intimate encounter with Soul to begin our relationship with it. In this book, we will first meet our own Souls, and then we can meet the Souls of others. The spiritual task before us is to allow Soul to live through us.

Every time we connect with our Soul, we accept it more; we reach deeper and deeper levels of intimacy with it. It is only in lis-tening to, adhering to, and having reverence for Soul's wisdom that we begin to fully understand ourselves. We all have access to our Divine nature, and once we acknowledge and accept this wisdom, we accept ourselves. We are wise, we are infinite, and we are Soul.

Elisa first met her Soul during an unexpected out-of-body experience. The meeting of her true self as Soul exposed her previous understanding of herself as ego. The following story helps illustrate that the Soul is not a mental concept or metaphor, but an always-available entity and connection to Holy Love.

Elisa Speaks

I had just left a daylong seminar at my depth-psychology graduate program school cotaught by two well-respected professors. I pondered the ideas they had discussed as I got my lunch. I started to feel light-headed when I sat down with my friends on the lawn to eat. My head had surprisingly begun to make slow figure-eight motions, as I felt my energy rising into my head and above my body. One friend, a skilled bodyworker and therapist, commented that it looked like I was entering into an altered state. He offered to hold energetic space for me in a private room. I completely trusted his integrity and ability to help me navigate whatever was starting to present itself. We left the group and went to my small private bedroom in the on-campus dormitory.

Almost immediately after I lay down on the bed, my consciousness, or where I was viewing the world from, flew up out of my body and hovered about three feet above it. I was shocked, experiencing myself *as myself*, but without the container of my body. I always had a fear that after I died and left my physical container, everything would cease to exist and fade to black. I had not dissolved or disappeared but felt shockingly the same. I looked down and, as consciousness, saw my physical self lying on the bed, wearing my bright turquoise shirt. I remember thinking how odd and dreamlike this was. I stayed there for a moment, disoriented.

And then I became aware of my true identity of Soul.

The feeling of my Soul was similar to how it feels to wake up from a vibrant dream. During the dream, there is a feeling that the experience is completely real, but when you awaken, there is a more clear understanding: "Oh, *this* is actually the dominant reality. *This* reality is more real than the dream reality." After meeting my Soul, I felt like I had woken up for the first time. Everything previous in the narrative of the life of Elisa Romeo felt *less* real and true than this newfound understanding and experience. I felt truly awake for the first time in my life.

It was at this moment of understanding that I was shown a vivid 3D movie of my entire life up until that point. Like a computer quickly downloading a large amount of information, I experienced this movie in a rapid way. I was receiving a complete and deep understanding of *why* all these seemingly random things had occurred, and at the same time I was experiencing them on an emotional level. I realized I was seeing my life from the perspective of my Soul, which was complete and total unconditional love. I could feel where She, my Soul, had always been rooting for the small (or egoic) me to choose the love option over the fear option in this choose-your-own-adventure life story unfolding on earth. The success or failure of my life was not through the achievements I had planned, but was actually dependent on my connection to making choices from love — which was ultimately about connecting with my Soul's presence. It was clear that the way to achieve true spiritual happiness and success — which was actually just honoring Her — was to listen to Her direction by consistently choosing love through the tests of life experiences on earth.

This was a shocking realization. So many moments in my life when I thought I was spiritually connected were purely mental (an *idea* of spirituality) and not *truly* connected to Her on a feeling and embodied level. Although I had felt alone, She had always been tethered to me by love. My spirituality had been built on the idea of being "good" or having a "high vibration" — *my idea of holy* — instead of submitting to my unique individual nature, which was created on purpose by love itself.

From my new vantage point, it felt sacrilegious or scandalous to continue to ignore Her presence in favor of the small will of my ego. With my narrow egoic blinders on, I had become habituated to looking for something that had never been hiding from me. I had a feeling of having missed the mark in much of my effortful trying at life, but She was actually as close as the next fully experienced deep breath. I did not feel met with judgment as I realized these things. I heard a clear and plain directive: *Please see this for what it is. You can trust and surrender into your nature.*

I understood how we agree to a form of spiritual amnesia as we enter into the experience of the personality (or ego) in order to play this game of life. It is almost like you need to completely enter into the Monopoly game or forget you are watching the feature film in order to enjoy and participate fully in them. If you are constantly stating, "This is only a game" or "This story doesn't matter, it's just a movie," it is hard to become submerged in and transformed by the experience. But at the same time, I saw how connecting to Soul helps us stay oriented to the reason we are here on a macro level and not drown in the frustrations and dramas on a micro level. It keeps us from losing ourselves completely to the game or story.

After I came back to my physical body, I felt completely disoriented. A Pandora's box had opened, and now I could feel, hear, and see the Souls of others calling for my attention. The feeling was like a weight of love bearing down on me to convey crucial pieces of love information. When I looked at other people, I could hear their Souls telepathically, as voices dictating sentences. I could see the energy of their Souls as a glowing golden ball two feet above their heads, connected by a cord down into their heart and surrounded by a sparkly white substance outside the aura. When someone said something from their heart, the golden tube above them lit up with energy; when they told a falsehood (that they may even have believed), their energy moved into the front of their forehead (the analytical mind) and kinked up the tube that was attempting to come down into their body from their Soul.

I was overwhelmed by this new sensory information; I had spiritual information overload. I felt a responsibility and urgency to clearly communicate the information of their Soul to the people before me. Sometimes, their Soul information was utterly in contrast to what they were telling me in our literal conversation. Many attempts failed as I tried to put words to my experience and was met with confusion, fear, apathy, or distrust. It rendered me completely anxious as I debated what the other person's Soul wanted me to communicate versus what would make my own human experience comfortable. I ended up essentially hiding in my parents' basement for a year while I tried to integrate this new energy and awareness. In this period of time, I felt like I was spending all my energy pretending to be human, acting egoic to fit in, while in truth I was feeling more identified with my Soul.

Yet this connection with my Soul opened a new communication line between us. Even though my new awareness made me appear socially phobic and awkward, I could hear Her urging me back into life. She was giving me daily instructions on how to integrate this fresh awareness in a helpful way and wanted to empower me as well as the people I was speaking to. I returned to my psychology internship. During sessions with clients, I built up my courage to begin to speak out loud what I was hearing their Souls urging me to communicate. After I delivered their Soul messages, clients would look at me, shocked, and say things like, "How do you know that? I have never told anyone that" or "You are putting specifically into words things I can feel but have never been able to express." Seeing the healing power of those messages gave me the courage to get out of my own way and use what this new gift had exposed for both myself and others.

I have a new orientation and interpretation of success now. True success is not about achieving anything in particular: ego comfort, creative projects, work triumphs, or financial goals. We may need to do these things in order to survive on earth, but they are not the ultimate point. The real objective is not the *what* of life but the *how*. Our true success comes from our intentions and attempts to know and partner with our Soul while we are here in the game of life. This is what builds embodied love consciousness. All real happiness comes from knowing, after you die, when you return home, that you consistently strove to choose love over fear by listening to, honoring, and consciously incarnating your Soul.

As we have discussed, Soul is known, not through the intellect, but through direct experience. It is now time for you to experience your own Soul. The exercise and meditation below are designed to facilitate a personal encounter with your higher self. Every meeting will look and feel different, as Soul's wisdom is perfectly tailored for what our ego needs to know on each specific day, in each specific moment. The most important thing to do is to drop any pressure, mental expectations, or perfectionism and stay open to the alive experience of what wants to be revealed.

Remember, Soul is your essence. Soul will feel like a familiar, yet often forgotten, part of yourself. When you meet your Soul, you will experience a feeling of recognizing and reclaiming the unconditional love that lives through you.

SOUL MEMORIES INQUIRY

Throughout our lives we have all had moments of feeling Soul. We often ignore or disregard them, because they may be subtle or easy to forget next to the constant demands life throws at us. We invite you to spend some time reflecting on the Soulful moments of your life.

- Describe a moment or period when you felt completely at peace.
- When was a time you felt utterly and completely accepted?
- Remember a time when you felt like you were part of something greater.
- Is there a time when you felt a deep sense of purpose? Have you ever felt like you were engaging in your inherent gifts and serving from that place? How did it feel? If you haven't felt this personally yet, do you have any ideas of things, activities, places, or people that might inspire this feeling within you?
- Daydream and list some times when you have felt your Soul. Soul is often known through a feeling of connection, a sense of purpose, or an experience of feeling loved, accepted, and a part of something greater.

MEDITATION: INTRODUCTION TO THE SOUL

An audio version of this meditation is available for free online at holyandhuman.com/holylove.

Find a peaceful place where you will not be disturbed or interrupted. For this meditation and prayer, you will need a comfortable chair or couch to sit on so you can easily sit upright with your feet flat on the floor. Sit with your legs and arms uncrossed. This is an active meditation, and you may receive intuitive information. You will also want to have a journal and pen nearby so you can take notes afterward. Do not have the writing materials in your lap but somewhere you have easy access to them.

We will begin this meditation with what is called box breathing, a breath pattern that has four parts. Sitting upright, first take a long exhale. Now inhale through your nose and slowly count to four in your mind. Feel the air filling your lungs until they are completely full. Now hold your breath and slowly count to four again. Exhale through your mouth and count to four as you feel the air expelling from your lungs and abdomen. Again, hold your breath out after the exhale, until you have slowly counted to four in your mind. Repeat the pattern: inhale through your nose once again while counting to four. Hold for four. Release the breath through your mouth for four, then hold the breath out for four. Take the next two minutes (feel free to use a timer) to find a natural rhythm with this cycle. If you like, you can imagine blowing out all anxiety and worries on the exhale and imagine receiving peace, goodness, and relaxation on the inhale.

Now, allow yourself to breathe naturally. Before we begin to connect with our Soul, remember that your Soul is your unique version of love. We all have an internal and eternal self, with its own individual nature. This is our highest self, our own version of grace, or our sainted self. We are now setting the intention to feel and connect with the fundamental essence that makes us who we are. We often feel separated from our Soul, interpreting who we are as an ego. This meditation will serve as an opportunity to quiet our minds and reconnect with this all-loving self.

If it's comfortable to do so, you may put one hand on your heart and the other on your belly, as this often helps to ground the exercise. On your next exhale, repeat the following phrases in your head: "I am ready to meet my Soul. I am willing to meet my Soul. I am ready to know my Soul. I am willing to know my Soul. I will know my Soul."

Now, imagine a wave of relaxation pouring over the crown of your head like water. This substance of relaxing water slowly trickles down the sides of your head and also within it. Imagine this relaxation pouring in and through your mind, soaking it in calm and peaceful energy. This water pours down even further, into your jaw, your throat, and your neck. Like a massage from the inside out and the outside in, like a salve for tension, this water of relaxation soothes all your muscles. Let the water flow down into your shoulders, releasing tension as it goes. Feel it flowing down your arms into your fingertips. Sense it flowing down your chest. As the water passes through your lungs and down to your stomach, allow it to slow your breathing to a peaceful pace. The water continues down through your hips, releasing any stored tension. And it continues to flow further down throughout your pelvis and down your legs. Imagine the water flowing all the way down to your toes, until your entire body is submersed in peace. Take a few moments to marinate in this state.

Beginning again at the crown of your head, allow the water of relaxation to pour through you once more. With each breath, imagine even more relaxation entering your body. This time allow it to put you into an even more relaxed state of peace.

After the water has washed over you a second time, imagine it once more, but this time flowing more smoothly and a little faster throughout your body. The water is no longer a trickle but a flowing stream. On your next inhale, imagine the water beginning again at your crown. With your next exhale, allow the water to travel all the way down your arms to your finger-tips, down your chest to your waist, and down your legs all the way to your feet.

Now, on your inhale, feel the water once again pouring through the crown of your head, and in a single exhale allow the water to flow entirely throughout your body, all the way down to your feet. Repeat this a few times at your own pace.

Now, take a few breaths naturally, without imagining the water, and just allow yourself to sit in silence. Repeat this prayer in your head: "Allow this moment to be filled with grace." With-out overthinking it, we are now going to imagine that the water is the substance of Divine love, grace in liquid form. On your next inhale, imagine the water of Divine love pouring into and through the crown of your head. Allow the water to seep down throughout every part of your body.

Now, return to normal breathing, without imagining the water. Turn your attention to your heart. You can place a hand or both your hands over your chest, if this helps. Imagine your awareness traveling deep into the center of your heart. You can imagine a downward staircase or a tunnel going deeper and deeper within. Once you have found the center, imagine there is an even deeper center, and a deeper center after that. Repeat this phrase in your mind: "I am willing to know my Soul. I will know my Soul."

Now imagine there is a small light in the deepest interior of your heart, like a light at the end of a tunnel. You are moving toward this light; it is slowly getting bigger and brighter. And mentally repeat this phrase: "I am willing to know my Soul. I will know my Soul." The light is getting brighter. You sense that once you have reached this light, you will know your Soul. Repeat this prayer: "Grace, enter my life now." Imagine the light growing bigger, until it is almost all-consuming. Repeat this phrase: "I am ready." As the light clears, ask your Soul to show itself to you, in a feeling, an image, or a phrase. You may repeat: "Soul, I am ready. How do you wish to make yourself known?" Now let go and allow Soul in.

When you are ready, open your eyes.

This is a great time to write down any information, imagery, or feelings you've just experienced. Just like waking from a dream, we may forget the experience very quickly as we change states of consciousness. Also, the experience may later seem unreal or foggy, so having a written account to reflect on will help you to integrate the new information.

CHAPTER 6

Hearing Soul's Wisdom

Put your ear down close to your soul and listen hard.
— ANNE SEXTON

When we are in conflict with our partner, it feels terrible: broken promises elicit betrayal, generosity of spirit turns to defensiveness, and a sense of belonging becomes desolation. Conflicts in relationship are unavoidable, and the way we deal with them is crucial. Some of us become masters at avoiding confrontation and vulnerability. Some of us continue to have faith in a more fulfilling love and persevere to try again. Most people find an in-between place, settling for a "take what you can get" attitude in the belief that all relationships are an awkward compromise. Soul offers a fourth solution: navigation from our Divinity.

Intuition is the voice of the Soul. Much of the work of navigating the Four Spiritual Relationships depends on our intuitive ability to clearly hear Soul's wisdom. Because the ego is quick to react or judge, it takes work, at times, to raise ourselves vibrationally to the love story of our intuition. And most of us live life as intuitive amateurs. We may occasionally receive clarity through a dream, a sudden feeling of unease, or a ping in our gut. But the skill of truly hearing and heeding Soul's wisdom requires becoming an intuitive pro. Instead of waiting for moments of intuition to come to us, we consciously build the intuitive muscle and learn to listen for specific answers to life's questions whenever we need to, even if we are stressed or in crisis.

Soul dialoguing occurs when we create a two-way dialogue between our ego voice and our Soul voice, out loud or in our head. We start by asking a question from our perspective as ego, and then we listen with our intuition to receive Soul's answer. Like any new skill, this may at first feel strange and challenging as our minds adjust to a different form of internal dialogue. But anytime we speak directly to Soul we strengthen the listening muscle of our intuition. Developing a relationship with Soul through intuitive dialogue helps the ego recognize, understand, and ultimately trust this new internal spiritual teacher. We believe the most efficient path to incarnating Soul is daily connection and practice with these techniques.

Soul dialoguing is a simple technique, but it also takes practice. To hear the voice of the Soul, we must be able to clearly discern what is ego (programmed narratives, society's influence, fears disguised as love) and what is Soul. Recognizing and listening to the Soul guarantees connection to and an experience of love but also shows us how *we are love* by birthright. Fully embodying the vastness of love is a process that takes time — but after we acquaint ourselves with our Divine nature, trust in our internal genius grows.

Real Love or Assumption of Love

Asking the Soul's advice, opinion, and direction brings Soul into our minds, hearts, and relationships. In applying Soul's wisdom, we strengthen our own ego-to-Soul bond and eventually develop conscious Soul communion with our partners. One of the simplest and most profound ways to speak to Soul is simply to ask yourself: "What would love say?" These four magic words harness the power of intention to activate our inner remote control and tune us in to the station of love. When you talk directly to love, you engage your unique version of love — in other words, your Soul.

Yet as humans we often misinterpret the internal voice of love. Depending on our upbringing, we may misinterpret needy attachment or codependency as love. We may think love and our self-worth are based solely on our ability to provide for our partner financially. We may think love is solving every single one of our partner's problems and consistently rescuing them from their own uncomfortable feelings. We may think love is staying in relationship till death do us part, even if we are desperately unhappy.

Soul corrects these misguided beliefs by introducing us to real love. Love is not fear based, clingy, or reactive; love is wholly and utterly complete, a force unto itself. To know love, we must take our human projections and limitations off love. We must come to the inquiry of love with an open heart, rational discernment, and a clean slate.

We know this sounds simple, but it can also be extremely challenging at times. In fact, we often see clients assume they are relating to their Soul when, in fact, they are engaged in an egoic interpretation or a mental assumption of Soul. This heady attempt does not work to actually solve the problems of the ego. Many times people think *about* the Soul and assume that because they are clocking "spiritual hours," they are engaging in a personal and direct relationship *with* Soul. But one is intellectualism, while the other requires vulnerability and courage. Talking *about* love is not the same as talking *to* love. When we talk to love, we engage directly with the universal energy that is birthing the incarnation of our sainted self. This is not a light task; it is one of destroying illusions. Ultimately our job is to weed out whatever stands in the way of love.

Soul dialoguing is a nuanced and disciplined approach to forging an intimate, accountable relationship with your higher self. When done correctly, it takes our own projections off love and reveals how love is greater than we could have ever fathomed. To do this well, we humble the ego, align with the energy of love, and become transformed by the Soul. This intimate relationship with love itself changes everything. There are no shortcuts. This spiritual skill relies completely on direct engagement with Soul. Soul must be accurately summoned to have its profound and lasting effects.

Love over Fear

The ego's nature is to blindly run ahead, assuming faster is better. As humans, our egoic wiring habituates us to work harder, not wiser. This is why we often state in sessions and workshops that the hardest part of talking to Soul is "remembering to remember." The ego needs to accept its limitations and remember to call upon the always available assistance of Soul.

When things are going well, it is easy to talk to love and hear the answers within. But when we are angry or feel abandoned by life, it is tempting to become stuck in a limited egoic perspective and become rigid or shut down. When we feel betrayed by our partner or the universe in general, the hardest part is to remember to directly talk, and listen, to love. In fact, it can feel excruciating to do so, and we may even lash out at well-intentioned people attempting to tether us back to love. When separated from Soul, the energy of love feels mocking. This Divinity litmus test reveals our biggest wounds with the eternal.

We simply need to remember to ask our Soul. Even though that sounds obvious, fear causes us to function from obsessive mental states, looking everywhere *but* Soul: *What do my friends and family think? What are my neighbors doing? What do the experts say? What are the results of the latest research?* In sessions, we've seen clients become stuck in endless ruminations over their pro-and-con lists, but when they just check in with the Soul and ask directly, the information is often incredibly accessible, clear, and shockingly apparent. All our life's answers are hidden in plain sight.

Hearing the voice of the Soul is one part intuitive training and one part courage. Employing intuition requires the courage to know what you already know. We used to think developing intuition would take clients years of meditation and training, but then we realized people often know exactly what they need to do — they just need the courage to admit it and surrender to it. For example, if a job or relationship is not working out or has become toxic, the person often fears and represses the intuitive information that would solve the problem. This only delays the inevitable reckoning.

Sometimes the fear of what we may hear keeps us from listening altogether. But if we have the courage to slow down and ask Soul, it always assists us on the journey to conscious love. So many of us have attachment wounds and fears, and we can find Soul information incredibly clarifying, useful, and healing. The following story from our client Harper is a great example of this.

Harper was aware intimacy triggered a stress response in her body, but she always assumed it would dissipate after she was in a long-term relationship. This did not turn out to be true. Harper had been married to Will for three years. Practically every time Will wanted to be intimate, her heart would begin to race. She trusted Will, more so now than when they first met, so she didn't understand why he activated so much fear in her. Her anxiety had only grown over time. After some practice with journaling, she asked her Soul for answers. Soul's blunt response was nothing short of miraculous in its insight: *You've never known love like this. You've never let someone in this deep before. You are beginning to realize how much you really love him and how much he loves you. This scares you. You don't want to love him unconditionally because you're afraid one day you might lose him. You're afraid of the pain that love may cause.*

Harper next asked how she could heal her fear. *You've been running from the pain*, Soul responded. *This causes a panic attack. Feel it, let Will hug you as you cry. Feel the pain and the love at the same time, and you will heal.* Harper used the ego-to-Soul relationship to consciously access what she had unconsciously suppressed. Harper and Will's intimacy has only grown since she made this breakthrough.

Connecting to Soul is not only a skill for adults. Children are often quite connected to their intuition, as they have not yet been trained out of it. Elisa had a session with a seven-year-old girl. Amelia was struggling with a bully at her small school. The ringleader of a group of girls had rallied the others against her. Amelia was scared of this mean girl clique and tried to avoid going to school. Her mother was concerned that Amelia had succumbed to their constant prods.

With some help, Amelia connected to her Soul. Elisa asked her to imagine an internal voice that was all-loving and all-knowing. Then, Elisa asked what advice Amelia's Soul might give her about the bully. In particular, she asked why these girls were picking on her and if there was anything Amelia could do to deter the teasing. It is often shocking how naturally this work comes to children. Amelia had swift access to the confident internal voice of her Soul: *The main girl is scared. Her parents are fighting at home, and she feels sad. She likes the feeling of being the boss.* To Amelia, the mean girls were instantly exposed for their own insecurities. Amelia no longer sounded like a seven-year-old but like a mature adult: "She says to not be scared," she reported to Elisa, "but also not to keep trying to play with them. To get them to stop, I just need to be me and find some other girls to play with instead." Amelia had heard her Soul information. She now knew how to act in her classroom with confidence. If Elisa had given her this information, Amelia wouldn't have felt the same sense of empowerment nor understood the minutiae of what Soul meant about how to be with these girls. With a slight refocusing on her internal truth, Amelia connected not only with her own Soul but with the Souls of the girls who had been tormenting her.

The intuitions and hunches we've known all along come from a deeper knowing beyond our default conscious state. With training, our minds can access this eternal information. Soul's information is often extremely pragmatic for navigating the ups and downs of any relationship. Where the ego needs comfort, connection, and answers, Soul responds. When we connect to Soul, we immediately levitate above the triggered or reactive pain we might be feeling and create an opening for healing. We align ourselves with a higher love than our pain can fathom and bring healing to old narratives. Where our minds lack solutions, Soul is a celestial genius.

Soul Journaling

Much like adding weights to a workout, Soul journaling takes Soul dialoguing to another level. Journaling is a particularly powerful way to connect to Soul. In fact, if we were to advocate for any one spiritual practice in this book, it would be regular Soul journaling. Although some people have a resistance to writing, we have seen incredible improvements just by adding this element to a client's practices. This consistent practice is the perfect way to hold ourselves accountable and expand consciousness between the ego and the Soul. It builds trust, communication, and understanding that is crucial for the ego-to-Soul relationship.

Soul journaling is a way to spend time with your Soul — the ultimate self-care date. Through the simple devices of paper and pen or a computer, we ask questions ranging from the seemingly small (Should I go for a walk today?) to the biggest imaginable (What is the meaning of life?). Because the practice is so straightforward and even obvious, we can be tempted to minimize its power. Yet this small action of sitting down and consciously setting the intention to hear directly from our Soul makes all the difference.

We suggest beginning with smaller and less intense questions as you start to build your listening muscle. If a question feels too overwhelming, it can shut down the progress you make in the beginning, so save the big questions for later, when you have a more established practice. Spending just five to ten minutes in the morning writing to our Soul can radically change our day. Instead of making a dozen decisions from stress or from mental ideas of what we "should" do, we begin to organize our day around our true purpose. Over time, the simple choice to ask our Soul's advice is life altering. From choosing the career that is most fulfilling to advice on raising our children, when we tune in to our Soul first, we make choices aligned with love that place us on our unique path to true happiness.

There are great benefits to physically writing down your Soul dialoguing. You create a document, a tool that allows the ego to review and integrate the information over time. Rereading our old Soul journaling is one of our favorite things to do. It brings us right back to our emotional state and consciousness level when the entries were written, and as we recognize the shifts that followed, it builds the trust the ego needs to learn to rely on the Soul and create a more conscious and intimate relationship. It becomes blatantly obvious, in hindsight, that the voice of Soul responding on the page is significantly wiser than the ego voice asking the questions. Particularly regarding old relationship questions that have now played out over time, the accuracy of the original Soul information becomes extremely apparent.

Soul journaling enables us to build our inner listening muscle through consciously changing our brain state. We all have five brain states, each having a purposeful function in our lives: gamma, beta, alpha, theta, and delta. Each of these states is defined by the amount, quality, and type of brain activity we are experiencing in the moment. These states also determine what we perceive and the type of knowledge we have access to. The gamma state is activated through tasks that require high levels of concentration, like studying for an exam or multitasking. Beta, our default daily state, is stimulated through focus on cognitive tasks and the external world. Alpha is activated when we enter a peaceful or contemplative state. Theta occurs most often in sleep, when we dream. And we enter the delta state in deep and dreamless sleep.

Theta is the state through which we can most easily access intuitive information. Although our brains automatically go into theta state when we're asleep, we can also purposefully access theta state while awake, through active imagination, meditation, and journaling. When we Soul journal, we enter theta state. Beta state may be essential for solving the more trivial tasks at hand, but theta state holds our wisdom and answers to life's bigger questions.

While Soul journaling, we learn to "go" somewhere in consciousness using our will and intention; the process is similar to getting in an elevator, pushing a button, and riding the elevator to the penthouse, the top floor with the best view. We raise our brain state, thereby raising our perspective, in order to get a higher view of the challenges and issues of our lives. The meditations in this book help facilitate the altering of brain state on command. Brain state travel takes a bit of time and practice to become second nature, so go easy on yourself in the beginning. Remember, you are learning a new, powerful, lifelong skill.

Because brain state changes are dramatic, it can be challenging to recall what specifically happened during the exchange with our Soul. Bits that are clear one hour after Soul dialoguing may be completely forgotten eight hours later. Writing the content down, during or immediately after the exchange, helps to clarify the power of what spiritually transpired.

Soul journaling is not only about receiving psychic or intuitive information. One of its hidden and most significant benefits is that it is also *a medium through which to integrate your Soul into your body*. Physical grounding and body healing take place when you move the energy of the Soul from the ethers, down the arm channels, and into a physical manifestation — in this case, through writing on paper or typing on a computer. Writing helps keep the ego grounded, focused, and on track instead of easily distracted by the next passing thought or strong feeling. When done correctly, Soul journaling is much more than a simple mental or information-based activity: it is a powerful form of energy work. By linking to and holding a conscious connection with the Soul, we create a vehicle through which true emotional and physical healing is possible.

Finally, the healing we create through Soul journaling is characterized by lasting psychological and spiritual integration. Other surface therapies, forms of energy work, meditations, or altered-state techniques may offer momentary relief and clarity, but ultimately the ego reverts back to its default personality functioning. Temporary results occur when the insights have not landed and become grounded in the emotional body. With Soul journaling, we thoroughly work through each egoic micro-resistance in real time. This practice evolves the ego, creating sustainable long-term results instead of simply providing momentary relief. The emotional integrative nature of Soul journaling is more challenging than some other, more passive energy techniques, but this is precisely why the results last. Soul journaling confronts the shadow and destroys spiritual bypassing. We see daily acceptance of egoic death and opening to Soul as *crucial* for success in the work of the Four Spiritual Relationships.

Because this work requires ongoing emotional presence, one could correctly assume that the biggest challenge of the practice is that it activates incredibly strong resistance in most people. This is not by chance. Great love activates great fear. It's often comical the degree to which people will go to avoid talking directly to their Soul. The ego can feel when the gig is up, and the personality begins to dance around the impending love. We beg for love to enter our lives, but often, when it appears, the ego reacts with protective reactivity and defensiveness. The places where inner gremlins of self-sabotage are hiding will be immediately exposed next to the powerful and transformational energy of love. Soul journaling summons all the unconscious death wishes right to the surface, exposing self-esteem issues and revealing where we have capped our receptivity to abundance. If we are asking the right questions, this practice can be threateningly confrontational to old, unhealthy ego thoughts and habits. We see this as an opportunity for Soul to wrestle with the ego on the mat.

Having a schedule of accountability or a goal of how many times a week you will journal can be particularly helpful to the ego, which may want to unconsciously retain power and control. If you notice you are regularly missing your sacred Soul appointments, the ego is likely unconsciously and actively resisting love. Ask yourself: Why would I avoid my Soul? Why would a little writing exercise be so incredibly daunting? Why would I not put in a bit of effort to check in with my true self? There really is no benefit to avoiding this part of ourselves. Ultimately, it is where all true happiness and success come from in life. Why would I leave my destiny to ego when I have the ability to hear my Soul?

On a purely practical level, Soul journaling is the most efficient way to align the details of your life with your higher self and deepest values. We see dramatic changes occur in our clients when they engage in consistent practice. When they are Soul journaling regularly five times a week, significant spiritual changes in the personality begin to occur. The ego loses its own agenda and becomes softer, more clear in its role as the hands and feet of Soul in the world. We often assign a schedule of Soul journaling five days a week for two weeks minimum, because it takes at least this much time to wrestle down the gremlins that initially surface. Once clients have conquered the energetic battle and reclaimed their spiritual authority, it becomes much easier.

As we often say, 80 percent of the success of Soul journaling is in asking the right questions. So what exactly are the "right questions"? To choose questions that significantly open the ego to love, you need to learn to tolerate the discrepancy of vibration between where the ego defaults and love's unconditionality. Begin by being excruciatingly honest about where you are emotionally — today, right now, in your life. If you are frustrated, angry, cynical, disheartened, or apathetic, start there. You need to emotionally address your relationship to the Divine to begin to get closer and trust it. If you do this well, we cannot think of a better investment in your life or a better way to use your time on the planet.

We find that Soul journaling is best understood when one can feel into the energy of other Soul journaling examples. Jane was in her final months of grad school. Stuck with writer's block, she was having a hard time finishing her dissertation. She talked with her Soul, named Grace, in her journal to get to the root of what was going on.

Jane: Why do I feel so weird and off today?

Grace: *You are putting too much pressure on yourself. You are [emotionally] flooding because you are over-whelmed. I know it feels like going backward, but you need to take time this morning to connect and center yourself. This will actually help you be much more efficient for the rest of the day.*

Jane: But why am I so stressed?

Grace: *The subconscious thoughts are that you need to prove yourself through your work. You are putting so much pressure on your dissertation to be amazing because you don't feel amazing yourself. Let your work be your work. Don't equate it with your true value.*

Jane: How do I feel better about my true value?

Grace: *Recite these mantras throughout the day and as breaks from your writing: "I am enough. I have nothing to prove. I am complete. I am love."*

The Soul journaling answers can, at times, be straightforward and obvious. Nonetheless, there can be something powerful and even radical in taking time to talk directly to the voice of love. It helps to hold the ego accountable and is a great way to check in and receive an expanded perspective on how life is going. Jonathan was growing tired of his bartending job. He lacked confidence but wanted to move toward his dream of purchasing a food truck and selling his delicious specialty sandwiches. He had saved up the money but was afraid to take the first steps. He wrote to his Soul, which he simply calls Happiness, in his journal for guidance.

Jonathan: OK. I'm tired of waiting for life to happen to me. Why am I so scared to make the leap?

Happiness: *You are always listing the worst possible things that can happen. You were trained by your family to be overly cautious. The worst thing is actually not trying. You feel you have a lot to lose, but really it is a great time to make this leap.*

Jonathan: Why does it freak me out so much to just do it?

Happiness: *You are making it bigger in your head than it really is. Don't let the anxiety freeze you — see your nerves as excitement. View this next chapter as an adventure.*

Jonathan: OK, so what is the next step?

Happiness: *Go see the guy selling the truck. Just call him up and go check it out. Bring Marty [Jonathan's best friend] for support. Once you get there, you will see that it is not as crazy of an idea as it seems. It will start to feel more doable. Just take one step at a time.*

Jonathan is currently living his dream in Portland selling his sandwiches. He looks forward to going to work these days and has a cultlike following for his grilled cheese paninis. (We have also benefited because they are truly delicious.)

Soul's wisdom increases our love to unknown heights. When we embody Soul's love through action, we become better people. True love's credo is simple: when we listen to the words and courageously act from Soul, we awaken to profound love in ourselves and each other. Soul journaling is the gateway to consciously embodying unconditional love.

But don't take our word for it. It's time to let your Soul speak for itself.

SOUL JOURNALING INSTRUCTIONS

Connecting to Soul is connecting directly to your core of love. By regularly practicing Soul journaling, you will align your external, physical life with the specific reasons you are alive on the planet.

Especially in the beginning, do not worry about how many of the details of your Soul journaling are accurate. First, concentrate on building the connection so you start to know and feel the "personality" of your Soul. Over time, your accuracy will naturally improve. This attitude takes the pressure of perfectionism off the ego and allows the natural healing energy work between ego and Soul to take place. Besides increasing our intuitive accuracy, remember Soul journaling is an opportunity to be *in* the energy of your Soul. We see the benefits that happen through Soul journaling as not only increased intuition but also powerful energetic healing. Think of it as Soul medicine.

You may write with a pen or pencil in a journal or type on the computer. (If you want to keep it private, you can always create a password-protected document or email entries to your own email account.) You can Soul journal first thing in the morning or in the middle of the night. Everyone is different, so see what works best for you. The best type of Soul journal is the one you are using!

Below we have included Soul journaling instructions and prompts. You can also find a printable version of these instructions online at holyandhuman.com/holylove.

1. **Name your Soul.** The Soul self is vastly different in identity and energy from the egoic self. Personifying the Soul helps the ego build a relationship to it and translate its powerful information. Avoid using your own name (so as not to confuse Soul information with egoic information) or the name of a friend or relative (to prevent connecting

with the wrong Soul). Don't be too worried about finding the perfect name for now. You can change the name later as you deepen the relationship. Here are three ways to name your Soul.

- **Pick a name.** Simply pick any name that represents your unique version of unconditional love. Often this is a name that feels loving, accepting, and inspiring. Again, this name can change over time.

- **Soul journal.** Pose the question in your journal, using Soul or Love as a placeholder. "Soul, what do you want to be called?" or "Love, what is your name?"

- **Meditate.** We have a free guided meditation, "Meet and Name Your Soul," on our website, holyandhuman .com/holylove. Use it to raise your brain state and ask your Soul directly for its name.

2. **Relax.** Meditating, jogging, or taking a bath can be great ways to prepare yourself to Soul journal. Anxiety is the greatest cause of Soul writing blocks. Find a peaceful place that is comfortable and a time you feel relaxed. It may help to put a hand on your heart to ground and calm your body.

3. **Set your intention.** Begin journaling with the intention to connect with your Soul. This is a pivotal step. Before you start journaling, take a moment to inhale and exhale deeply, relax, and set your intention.

4. **Just ask.** Begin with questions that aren't too emotionally charged or stress producing. Do not begin with questions that try to "prove" or validate the Soul's information to the ego. You can warm up to these questions as you grow your practice and faith. For now, it's best to keep your mind in a state of receiving information.

5. **Start where you are.** The most common reason people get stuck with Soul journaling is because they are

avoiding the question that is emotionally up for them in the moment. To learn to wrestle on the mat emotionally, just honestly admit where you are and start there. Ask the questions weighing on your heart right now. For example, if you think you can't hear your Soul's voice clearly, ask what is going on. First, identify your feeling (see figure 6 on page 100) and then ask love's wisdom how to process and work with that feeling.

6. **Ask the right questions.** Again, 80 percent of effective Soul journaling lies in asking the right questions. Lead with questions that address your emotional needs first to bring relief and avoid freezing your process. Then move on to questions that are more practical and focused on life information. If any information triggers anxiety or fear, stop and refocus your questions on what you need emotionally right now. This will allow you to stay in theta state for receiving guidance.

7. **"If I pretended to know..."** In this practice we will be moving back and forth between states of consciousness. This requires we leave our rational, self-critical minds at the door; it's best to be playful, not too hard on ourselves, and to leave plenty of room for mistakes. A beginner's trick to getting the Soul to respond is simply to pretend. We often use the phrase "Fake it till you make it." If you are stuck and not receiving information from your Soul, pose this question: "If I pretended to know what love would say, what would it be?"

8. **What does love say?** As we noted earlier, there is a huge difference between talking *about* love and talking directly *to* love. This practice is your opportunity to speak to and hear from love. Don't overthink what is happening; just be open to how love wants to bless your life. Though the information may not necessarily be what you want to

hear, it will always be said in a compassionate voice. If the answers that come back are critical, shaming, or perfectionistic, it is not your Soul speaking.

9. **Stick with it.** Like with any relationship, it takes time to get to know your Soul. Having scheduled times when you plan to journal can help the ego to build Soul accountability. At first, you may mistake intuitive information for what you *want* to hear or what you think you *should* do. As with any skill, you will get better at identifying Soul's voice if you persist. Here are some signs to help you recognize Soul versus ego information:

- **Voice.** Over time, you will notice a difference between the writing voice of your egoic questions and the voice of your Soul's answers. Clients have described their Soul's voice as being anywhere from eloquent and poetic to unapologetically direct and confident. It will be reflective of your unique Soul's personality.

- **Accurate intuitive information.** You may start to get psychic information that your ego would not otherwise have access to. A common mistake at this phase is to assume, after you've gotten one accurate psychic answer, that all answers will be correct thereafter and then to be disheartened when you get a miss. Think of yourself as being like the basketball player who has gotten the ball in the hoop several times but may still not be playing at NBA level. Consistency takes practice.

SOUL JOURNALING PROMPTS

One way you can demonstrate your commitment to your Soul is by getting a beautiful journal that feels like your Soul and dedicating it to this practice. Here are some suggested writing prompts you can use to start to talk to your Soul.

- How am I doing? What's going on with me emotionally and energetically in this moment? [If you feel resistance, often the Soul work is to consciously be with and feel the emotions that are surfacing, to breathe through them, and to continue on.]
- Where am I connected to you, and where am I disconnected, avoidant, or defensive? Is there a reason that I am resisting your energy or information? If so, how can I feel less resistant and more calm and safe? What percentage am I disconnected versus connected to Soul? What percent am I hearing you clearly right now?
- Am I carrying any misguided beliefs that are blocking my ability to hear you? What are they?
- What am I doing well? How do I naturally connect to Soul?
- What do you want me to know right now?
- What do you want me to do today? Is there anything you would add or change about my schedule?
- How did I do in journaling today? What percentage was Soul coming through?
- Is there anything I should know for next time?
- What does my Soul feel about this Soul journaling session? What was happening energetically between my Soul and my ego?
- What's one thing I can do to help myself stay connected to Soul today?

CHAPTER 7

Healing the Inner Child

Instead of transcending ourselves, we need to move into ourselves.
— MARION WOODMAN

In the last chapter, we discussed how to use the ego-to-Soul re-lationship to receive intuitive information. After connecting to the voice of Soul, we go deeper into the crevices of subconscious habits and transform them with healing acts of Soulful self-love. For any relationship to thrive, we need to be accountable, able to clean our side of the street by tending to our own inner wounds or abandonment issues. In this chapter we show you how to create a foundation of self-care and insight in order to be successful in all your relationships.

Ironically, refocusing from the other in our relationship to our own Soul increases the depth of intimacy possible between our Soul and another. We become strong in our inner knowing and freed from dependency on anything external for direction or sense of self. This is the "work" part of Soul work in this book, so be patient with yourself and feel free to take it slowly or come back to this section repeatedly over time.

The Inner Child

What we have learned from years of working with couples is that relationships thrive to the degree that each partner takes responsibility for healing their own inner child. The inner child is a subpersonality formed from our experiences and memories, both good and bad, and lives within the subconscious mind. At times this inner child can be full of wonder, playful and creative in ways our adult self has forgotten. Other times this child rages, cries, and lashes out with a lack of emotional maturity.

We can see this child surface in ourselves (or others) when an event triggers our childlike emotions. Our happy inner child may be activated during a moment of nostalgia. We may suddenly feel a spark of childlike joy when we hear the familiar song of an ice-cream truck, a cozy warmth as we enjoy hot cocoa in the winter, or an innocent sense of awe while exploring tidal pools at the beach. When we access this part of ourselves, we experience a simple purity. It is important as adults that every so often we allow time for our inner child to play. Childish play helps us break through the monotony of our responsibilities and cultivate joie de vivre. When we bring our childlike wonder to our relationships, through activities that makes us laugh and allow us to let our guard down, it creates an atmosphere of safety, amusement, and optimism.

But the same inner child that can bring joy can also bring emotional chaos into our lives, including our relationships. When we are highly reactive, impulsive, and lacking in the ability to regulate our emotions, it is likely our wounded inner child is activated. When we were young, we didn't always have power over our own lives or the ability to take care of ourselves. The wounded inner child can feel abandonment, helplessness, rage, unworthiness, and fear; their lack of power can make dangerous or hurtful experiences from childhood feel that much more traumatizing. Of course, we can go through any of these emotions as adults, but what defines an inner-child activation is a quality of regression and immaturity.

If an attachment wound occurred at the age of six, then our internalized angry six-year-old will pop into our next fight seeking attention, rebellion, or vengeance. We may shout something like, "If you don't like the way I do things, then I don't like you!" Our composure quickly breaks down when our inner child is triggered, and our reasons for being mad become more and more unreasonable.

The inner child can also manifest internally in the form of an overly dramatic and illogical narrative. Inner-child emotions are often absolutist, riddled with rigid black-and-white thinking. Thoughts like "I'm not good enough, no one likes me," "I'm broken and will never be fixed," and "Everything is my fault" lack the nuanced discernment of an adult mind. For example, an adult may understand that we may make mistakes and it doesn't mean we are a bad person, while our inner child may be trapped in a shame spiral. Fortunately, we can actively reparent and heal these impaired parts of ourselves. With self-love comes emotional maturity.

Reparenting may not sound like something mature adults would need to do, but if your inner child feels wounded and ignored, it is guaranteed to become needy and overly demanding in your current relationship. If you need proof, just watch a little reality television, where wounded inner-child behavior is at an all-time high. There would be little drama in the reality-TV world if these handpicked participants (most likely chosen for their lack of emotional maturity) did not unravel into their highly reactive and unreasonable childhood selves when faced with conflict. While this makes for dramatic television, in relationship such behavior is horrible for connection, communication, and intimacy. It is well worth our investment of time and energy to become conscious of our inner wounds, thus helping our current relationships flourish.

Our own inner child stays immature because of internalized self-judgment or a feeling of unworthiness. These wounds carry with them an unconscious belief that we do not deserve to be healed in the first place, which makes it challenging to treat our inner child with patience and compassion. We convince ourselves that our own feelings are pointless, foolish, a waste of time, or irrelevant. By minimizing our feelings, we compartmentalize and cut off our inner child. Building a healthy ego-to-Soul relationship is helpful here, as it enables us to reconnect our inner child to our own source of clarity and higher love.

Whenever we connect to our Soul, it is an action of self-love. We access the part of our being that is capable of endless compassion and understanding. In the words of the Sufi poet Rumi, "Only the soul knows what love is." Though our ego may imagine it has a fairly good grasp on love and self-compassion, its perceptions remain filtered through our emotional wounds and sense of egoic worthiness (or lack thereof). We cannot heal our inner child from the vantage point of the child. We must find within ourselves the all-loving parent — the internal voice that never gives up on us, that is always kind and forgiving, that provides sage wisdom from the heart. This internal voice is the Soul. Though it may be difficult to imagine or accept, all the love we ever needed is already within us.

Thus the ego-to-Soul relationship encompasses the relationship between our inner child and inner all-loving parent. When we dialogue with our Soul, we hold space and compassion for the ego as we would for our own child. When we are upset, overwhelmed, anxious, or scared, we allow the egoic voice to speak these feelings into awareness, where the Soul meets and heals them with unconditional love.

Our client Mike used Soul journaling to help himself reparent an abandonment wound from his mother. His wife's name is Claire; his Soul's name is Big Love.

Mike: I can't think straight. My body is shaking. Why am I so worked up?

Big Love: *You feel as if Claire is leaving you. This is not true. She is upset with you for not listening to her last night, but she loves you. Take a breath. You are safe.*

Mike: But why am I so scared? I can't calm down.

Big Love: *Place a hand on your heart. Imagine yourself wrapped in love. Slow your breath. Claire will not leave like Mom did. She will be there for you. She just needs time to cool off. Talk with her in the morning. Instead of showing her your anger, show her your fear and vulnerability. Communicate why you are afraid.*

Mike: I don't understand, what should I say?

Big Love: *Tell her, when she is upset, you are afraid she will leave you. Bring this wound to the light of day, and it will lose its power. Talking about it will give Claire an opportunity to prove her love to you, and it will prove to yourself that your wound is not true. You do not need to make people happy for them to love you. Your love for each other is greater than this wound. Once you truly understand this, you will begin to heal.*

With the help of his Soul journaling, Mike was able to identify the internalized wound from his past instead of taking it out on his spouse. He was able to communicate his fears the following day and work through them with Claire. A situation that could have escalated and created more distance in the relationship ended up strengthening their bond. Later, Claire told us that since Mike had become aware of his abandonment wound, he was less reactive and more responsive to her. Before she had felt there was no space for her own emotions in the relationship, because expressing them would often set off Mike's insecurities. Now, their relationship is more dynamic and healthy; it has room for growth.

It may be hard to imagine our internal all-loving parent because many of us never had models of one growing up. We believe the patron saint of healing inner-child work is Mister Fred Rogers. If you grew up in the 1970s or '80s, you may have fond memories of his popular children's show, *Mister Rogers' Neighborhood*. This groundbreaking show approached children with an inherent respect, honoring their emotional complexity and ability to handle difficult topics such as divorce and death. What we learn from Mister Rogers is that Holy Love does not need to be complicated. Rogers's simple phrase "I like you just the way you are" is the platform of self-acceptance required for all the challenges of life. Rogers himself captures the Divine significance of love perfectly. He once said, "I believe that appreciation is a holy thing — that when we look for what's best in a person we happen to be with at the moment, we're doing what God does. So, in loving and appreciating our neighbor, we're participating in something sacred."

Ideally, a parent loves a child unconditionally, "just the way they are." As parents, obviously we still encourage our children to acquire new skills or reflect to them the areas where they can improve. But the inherent connection with and ability to see their Soul is reflected through the quality of the relationship. Through our relating, we send the silent message that our love for our children is not dependent on their actions or abilities. We love them no matter what. This is the same inherent love we are attempting to activate through cultivating our ego-to-Soul relationship.

We stand on sacred ground when we learn to love ourselves so purely and directly. We all have an intuitive sense that there is a deeper character within us, the person we were always meant to be. This is the Soul, which is up against all our inner self-doubt, false identifications, and self-criticism. The paradox is, we never have to change ourselves to embody our Soul self — we need to change only the way we love ourselves. Self-love creates the opening in our hearts for our Soul nature to come through. Soul dialoguing is our get-out-of-jail-free card. We no longer have to find out who we are through comparison, cultural circumstance, or the stories of our past; we receive that knowing through the direct wisdom of our own Soul.

THE FEELING CHART

The first step in reparenting our inner child is to build a strong ability to clearly identify our feelings in the moment. Take five minutes a day for one week to bring awareness to your feelings and identify three of the emotions from the feeling chart (figure 6) each time. After you have identified your feelings, you can decide if you need to "do" something about them or just allow them to be. It's important to bring curiosity, compassion, and awareness to your present emotional state.

Warning: this simple exercise is more powerful than it appears! We have found that identifying three feeling words is much harder than most people would think. Oftentimes, we run through the day on autopilot and ignore our feelings. When we're asked in earnest, "How are you feeling?" it is common to reply with "Fine" or "Good," which actually are not true feeling words.

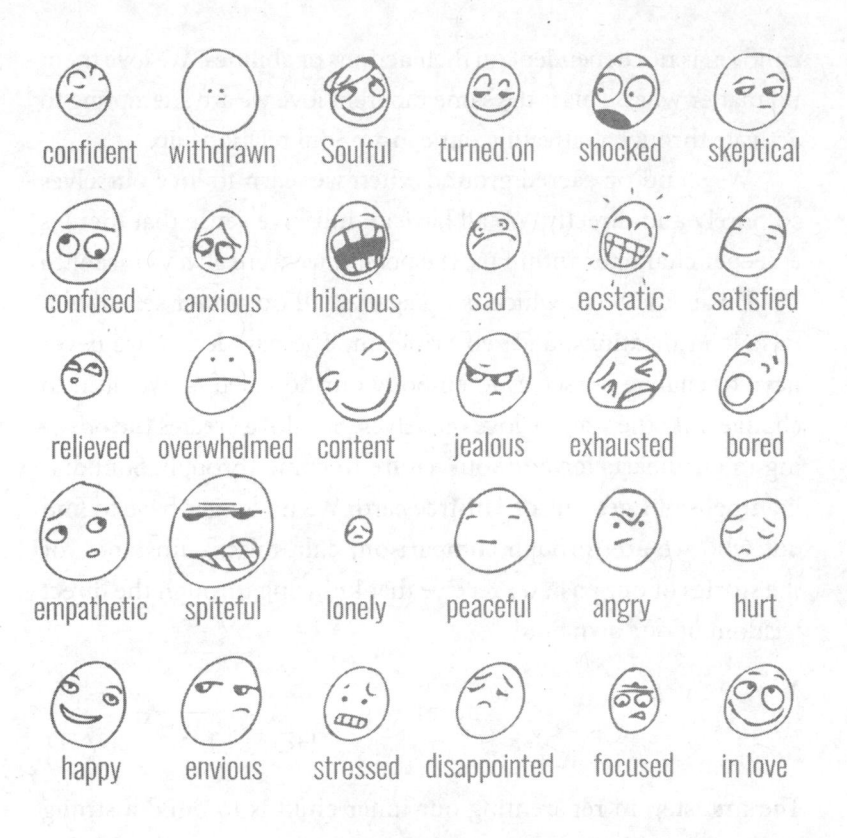

Figure 6. The feeling chart

SOUL JOURNALING PROMPTS FOR THE INNER CHILD

Find a comfortable place to Soul journal where you won't be interrupted. Take a few deep breaths and set the intention to bring love and healing to your inner child where it is needed. If it helps, visualize you are an all-loving parent speaking with your childhood self. Then ask:

- How does my inner child feel right now?
- What does my inner child want to tell me?

- What can I do for my inner child today?
- Is there any wound I need to work on? If so, how?
- What would my inner child enjoy?
- Is there anything I need to communicate from my inner child to my partner?
- Is there anything you, my Soul, want to tell me about my inner child?
- How can I bring more self-love into my life?

INNER CHILD PLAY DATE

Spend an afternoon or a whole day doing whatever your inner child wants. As adults, we always have responsibilities and time pressures, which can stunt our imagination and suck the joy out of our inner child. Set some special time aside to make your feelings a priority and find activities (or lack of activities) to nourish them. Surround yourself with comforting and even childlike things to explore and play with. Find some watercolors to paint with, put on some music to dance to, prepare a long bath strewn with rose petals, or spend some time wandering in nature. Create a day with no time pressures to really explore what you naturally feel like doing. What would help you spark wonder and bring you joy today?

One suggestion may be to watch Mister Rogers, as he is the patron saint of permission to feel your feelings. We highly recommend the HBO documentary *Won't You Be My Neighbor?* As an additional step, you could even think of something currently troubling you and imagine what Mister Rogers might say back to you.

For those doing deep inner-child work, it significantly furthers your relationship with your inner child to create a little shrine in your home. Find a childhood photo and some sacred objects that remind you of how you felt when you were young.

This space becomes a place to meditate, to feel and process old wounds and memories, and to reparent yourself the way you wish you had been treated. Your shrine serves as a visual reminder to treat yourself with compassion and speak to yourself with kindness, just as you would if you were still that innocent young child.

INNER CHILD AFFIRMATIONS

Affirmations are a wonderful tool to help you reparent and heal your inner child. Affirmations can be written in your journal, spoken aloud with conviction, or repeated as a mantra in meditation. The following are some suggestions. Feel free to use these or make up your own, specific to what your inner child needs to hear to feel loved and appreciated.

- I am allowed to take the time to feel my feelings.
- It is OK to make mistakes.
- I am allowed to not know all the answers.
- I give myself permission to play and explore.
- I am allowed to say no to the people, places, and things that do not serve me.
- I deserve to take the time for self-care.
- I am worthy of love.
- I am safe.

CHAPTER 8

Tough Love

*Boundaries are the distance at which I can
love you and me simultaneously.*

— PRENTIS HEMPHILL

While Soul is always loving in its intention and delivery of
messages, Soul also always sees and speaks the truth, even
if it is uncomfortable. Soul understands that when the people we
care about are stuck in habitual unhealthy behavior, communicating loving observations, clear boundaries, or disappointing
feelings is required. Instead of tiptoeing around hard truths when
there's interpersonal conflict, we trust the inherent love of the relationship to sustain us. And sometimes, we have to hurt an ego
to love a Soul.

One of the most common blocks to spiritual intimacy we see
in relationships is a lack of discernment between what is love and
what is actually codependency. Many people think *codependency*
is a term that applies only to vulnerable people who are enabling

an addict in their lives. Yet codependency is much more common and nuanced than the classic understanding suggests. We find it is essential to understand a bit about codependency in order to successfully navigate the terrain of Holy Love.

Codependency occurs when fear leads us to ignore our truth and to put the feelings and beliefs of another person higher than our own Soul values. Codependency, though unhealthy, is often born from an attempt to love. Some of the most empathic, loving, and sincere people get caught in emotionally abusive relationships because of codependency issues. Because its energetic origins are fear based, such a love is actually flimsy and false, incapable of providing true support for growth.

When we are in a codependent relationship over a long period of time, we can slowly lose touch with our inner reality. In severe codependency, we become attached to and benevolent toward the perpetrators in our lives. We may become convinced that emotional manipulation or abuse is love and affection. Yet codependency can also be much more subtle, serving as a defense mechanism or manifesting in minor but impactful miscommunication in our relationships. We saw this recently with a couple in a session.

Nia had been wearing the engagement ring Tyler gave her for only twenty-four hours. This was what she had always dreamed of — she had secretly hoped that Tyler would pop the question for a while — so she didn't understand why she was having a panic attack. Nia told us, "I just felt scared. I didn't know why. I thought this man couldn't really want to spend the rest of his life with me. He must be lying or something. I guess I was waiting for the other shoe to drop."

Tyler could feel his new fiancée's overwhelm. This was not the romantic experience he expected. It was not hard for him to interpret Nia's reaction as doubt in her feelings toward him. He assumed she was regretting her answer. Though all he wanted was to marry her, he also did not want to show his true feelings and vulnerability.

So instead of expressing his love, Tyler expressed a trained codependency, which stemmed from a fear of rejection. In an attempt to not pressure Nia and "scare her away," he told her that if she was anxious, they could put off the wedding; it was "no big deal" to him. His fear of expressing the vulnerability of his desire — his real Soul truth — caused him to subsume himself in Nia's apprehension.

Needless to say, Nia's panic was validated: she now believed he did not take the idea of marriage to her seriously after all. Tyler's codependency led him to misread the situation and misinterpret his fiancée's sadness. As soon as we submit to codependency, our mind searches for the quickest fix to end the uncomfortable situation. We quickly get lost in a sea of emotional empathy and can miss the resolution our Soul is directing us to.

In a couples session, Tyler was able to connect to his Soul, surmount his codependency, and tell Nia how he truly felt. He expressed his deep desire to be with her along with his total confidence about wanting to spend every day together for as long as they could. She was filled with relief. Her anxiety subsided within moments, and they began to celebrate their impending union.

From his new Soul vantage point, Tyler described their miscommunication: "It was like her fear was feeding my fear, and mine was feeding hers." When we connect to Soul, we have the opportunity of transforming our relationship from fear to love. When we do not, we can accidentally escalate a cycle of pointless misunderstandings for a lifetime.

The term *codependency* was initially attributed to individuals in relationships with addicts, as we mentioned earlier. Loving an addict is a complicated and painful process. Sometimes simple supportive love is not enough. If you love an addict, you have to be crystal clear where their addicted self may be actively sabotaging their success in life and blocking their connection to their Soul.

Lines need to be drawn and strong boundaries set in order to uphold the love that is required during these tough and testing times. Putting up healthy boundaries can be heartbreaking. Tough love can often feel unkind and even cruel. But if we are trapped in codependent behaviors, like denial and enabling, we cannot help our partner. When we can remember the boundaries we are setting are with *the addictive energy itself* and not the Soul we love, we are more readily able to hold our partner accountable.

Hints of codependency may be found in a wife's obsessive focus on her husband's mood or a child's fixed obligation to a mother's narcissistic needs. In short, *codependency* may be defined as "how I feel depends on how you feel." The need to be approved of, accepted, or seen outweighs the individual's connection to their own inner truth. Often stemming from attachment issues, this happens when we need approval from the other person more than the connection and feeling from our own Soul. We are all somewhat affected by the feelings of others around us, but if we are tyrannized by a loved one's issues at the expense of our own emotions, we've dimmed our light and our connection to Soul. If we continually make fear-based instead of love-based decisions in a relationship, it is a sure sign codependency is a factor. But if we listen to Soul, we can break the pattern and open into a wider vista of love. Only a small and fragile love keeps us stuck in codependent cycles.

When we connect to the unconditional love of Soul, we receive incredible strength and perspective. Soul understands the highest good of all people involved, always. Sometimes love is direct and relentless in its unwavering commitment to true

connection. Soul is a master at the complicated art of loving another person. Soul knows that our loved ones sometimes need a
hard-ass coach speaking an uncomfortable truth in a loving way.

When Loving Is Leaving

Joy had been married for twenty-five years to a narcissist. A part
of her knew from the beginning something was wrong in her relationship. She felt it instinctually as a passing thought and a sadness in her heart, but she was unsure what was true. As the years
went on, Joy began to realize her husband frequently lied to and
manipulated her. The untruths started out as white lies but over
time became much more obvious and damaging. He was obsessed
with power and his own self-importance in an unbalanced and
emotionally harmful way. He was a master at subtle and not-so-
subtle techniques to maintain control of the relationship and control of her. Joy had married a narcissist.

Joy shared with us the hardship of loving a narcissist:

Honestly, I've known this for so long, from the beginning
of our marriage. But I never allowed myself to go in there
and feel it because I was afraid. He controlled my life to
such a depth, I couldn't even imagine trying to take control myself. Whenever I had a conversation, I never knew
if this was a lie or manipulation or real. Every conversation we had was to make him feel right or larger. To fulfill
his need to be better than me, to have power over me.

Whenever I told him how I was feeling, he would just
change the story through his lens. I began to doubt myself
more and more and lose touch with what was true to me.

Then, Joy met her Soul and opened the communication line
to her intuition. She began Soul journaling daily and could now

clearly hear the voice of those unsettling instincts she had felt for years. At first, Joy focused on the rehabilitation of their relationship. She asked her Soul questions like "Can this relationship be changed?" "Is there anything I can do to bring out the best in my husband?" and "Can I help heal his narcissism?"

Soul answered but with an unexpected solution. Joy came to realize that helping her husband face his narcissistic patterns and healing her own wounds would be achieved only by her leaving. If she made this painful choice, he would no longer have control over her. He would have to face a reality he had been avoiding for twenty-five years — he never had control over her Soul. She knew this would cause both of them suffering, but it was clear from the unconditional love of her Soul that this decision held the most healing potential for them and their family.

Since leaving her husband, Joy has blossomed into a strong and confident woman who is now discovering the vividness of life being lived on her own terms. "I feel clear for the first time," she says. "There is a joy in the clarity. It makes me feel strong and have a trust within myself."

Her relationship to her children and grandchildren has opened to new possibilities as well. Joy describes it this way: "As I was playing and interacting, I noticed how much more open and happier I was. My head was not cluttered with stress, thinking about what my husband wanted from me. I was free, clear, and open to just be in the moment and take in totally who my granddaughter and children really are."

We recently received an email from Joy that is a testament to her inner work and progress. "I am not even sure how I got to this point," she wrote, "but for the first time in my life I am no longer emotionally controlled by another human being. That is true freedom! I really feel good, incredibly strong, peaceful, and know I can make the right decisions and choices for myself along the way!!" It can be heartbreaking to receive guidance from Soul to

leave a relationship behind. Even though we may be aware it is necessary for our own healing and perhaps even the most loving way
forward for all involved, we may still feel guilty about abandoning
others. It is helpful at these times to remember what the path of
consciousness entails. Consciousness is awareness of what love is
and is not: we become aware that our beliefs and actions are coming from fear instead of love. This growing consciousness can be
unsettling, but if we choose to ignore it, we will have to exert extra
energy to repress the newfound knowing. Pretending to not know
what you are now aware of is an exhausting task. Repression saps
up vital energy that could be better used nourishing our new Soul-
aligned life; it halts our growth. When we finally acknowledge what
we've been denying, we disengage from our internal battle and are
free to expand into the whole of our awareness.

In his memoir *Memories, Dreams, Reflections*, the pioneering
Swiss psychiatrist Carl Jung likened this process to being on a battle-
field for consciousness. On our journey toward consciousness, a
fellow comrade might fall. This could be a friend, family member,
or other loved one who falls prey to addiction, trauma, neurosis,
or any wound that brings their personal growth to a halt. Because
of their wounds, our comrade cannot go on. If we stay by their
side in their final hours, while the battle rages on around us, we
may also perish in the shrapnel of unconsciousness. It is likely
then to be the end of our own journey as well. Yet, if we choose
to continue our journey instead of sacrificing ourselves, we must
face the heartbreaking grief and guilt of leaving behind someone
we love.

Do we sacrifice our own well-being and tend to the wounds
of our comrade? Or do we allow ourselves to experience the pain
of heartbreak so that we can survive and live to love another day?
We appreciate that this is not a simple hypothetical. Jung recognized that by leaving someone behind, we may appear uncom-
passionate. And even if it is necessary for our well-being to leave,

doing so may cause us great grief. Jung understood that sometimes the most loving choice is a painful one, but ultimately a choice we must make anyway. If we choose to stay, we may be sacrificing our chance to fulfill our intended destiny.

Even though leaving can be initially painful, codependency within a relationship causes a unique kind of loneliness that usually lasts much longer. When our relationship is stuck in this unconscious no-man's-land, we feel alone even when we are with our partner. When we trade our Soul's truth for codependency, we feel unseen, unheard, and ultimately unloved. If we are incapable of claiming our truth, our authentic selves remain hidden, unavailable for real intimacy. Part of the journey of Holy Love and Soul communion is to be honest with ourselves, and others, about what our Soul's truth is.

Truth Breaks Us Open to Soul

Soul's love is always unconditional, but that love may show up in many different ways. At times it may be socially appropriate, but at others, it is unbridled. In one moment Soul's love may take the form of a hug and a long conversation, but in the next, it may roar like a mama bear protecting her cubs. Love shows anger and even expresses feelings of betrayal when the people we care about are suffocating their connection to Soul and harming themselves. This frustration does not come from an egoic reaction but from a commitment to the higher Soul lessons and love contracts. Every Soul-fueled emotion, even difficult ones, emerges from deep wisdom and a sincere hope for everyone's ultimate healing.

We can rest in comfort knowing the opposite of codependency is clarity in one's own authentic Soul. Soul does not live within a set of rules — who we "should" be, how we "should" act, what we "should" or "should not" say. In fact, identifying as "a spiritual person" often gets in the way of Soul truth. Spiritual perfectionism has caused many people to ignore their intuition in favor of a set of abstract rules because of the belief that "a spiritual person would do this" or "a spiritual person would never do that." To radically listen to Soul, we must leave behind *all* conventions of who we "should" be to discover who we were all along. This means letting go of the egoic need for approval and setting free the untamable nature of our truth.

We may be afraid of hurting the people around us — and ourselves — if we claim our Soul's truth. But in the end, Soul truth is where love resides. As long as we keep ourselves separated from what we really want and need, we rob ourselves of the opportunity to know, and show, the meaning of unconditional love.

We cannot predict the consequences of speaking our Soul's truth. Truth may cause pain; truth may birth a new appreciation for another; truth may break our relationship; truth may lead us away from another, only to bring us back later; and truth may inspire a union for a lifetime. No matter the immediate consequences, Soul truth always leads us to a life of authenticity, a confidence in ourselves, and a love beyond measure. We tell ourselves many stories, but only the Soul has access to the full story of the truth. Every day when we dialogue with Soul, we strengthen the inner connection to truth; and truth, as we have said, is the first step to true love.

TOUGH LOVE INQUIRY

This Soul dialoguing inquiry investigates the subtle or overt ways that codependency can hide in a relationship. Codependency is fear-based love; it is unconscious love that does not know itself. Talking to Soul is the best way to transform codependency into consciousness. Asking your Soul for information, let's begin to transform codependency into clarity and love.

- Is there anything in my relationship I've been avoiding saying?
- If so, why? What am I afraid of?
- Is this a realistic fear? What will be the likely outcome if I say it?
- Is there a way my Soul wants me to say my truth? Any specific words or phrases it wants me to use?
- Are there any ways I feel responsible for others that come from codependence and not from my Soul?
- Are there any relationships, or behavior within my relationships, that are energetically and emotionally draining? Are there any of my own values, needs, or boundaries that I have been denying or avoiding?
- Is there anything Soul wants to tell me about how to clear any codependency in my current relationships?
- Are there any ways I have been carrying problems for others that I can shift into support of those people instead of codependency?
- How can I bring more Holy Love into my relationships?

RELATIONSHIP CHECK-IN INQUIRY

Most couples do not talk about their relationship issues unless the issue itself is currently up. But it is during times of conflict, stress, and emotional overwhelm that we are the least capable of hearing and understanding each other. Try scheduling a time when you both are relaxed and in a good place in your relationship to sit and talk about how things are going. Make sure to talk about what makes you strong as a couple as well as about the issues you would like to work on. Here are some questions you can ask each other to open up discussion:

- What is something you love about me?
- What do you think are our strengths as a couple?
- What is something you appreciate that I do for you?
- Is there any area in the relationship where you feel unseen or unmet?
- If so, what is something I could do to help make this better? (Make it a practice to provide positive solutions.)
- Is there anything you think we are avoiding talking about as a couple?
- [Take a moment for you both to connect to your Souls.] Is there anything your Soul wants to say to mine? Is there anything Soul wants us to start doing for each other?
- How do you like for me to show my love for you? What specific words or actions do you enjoy?

CHAPTER 9

Meet Their Soul

As long as we're doing the work,
it might as well be the kind that lasts forever.

— RICK RUBIN

While reacquainting ourselves with our Soul reminds us of our internal Divine nature, the third spiritual relationship — the ego-to-their-Soul relationship — allows us to see the Soul nature in another. Seeing the Soul of another builds our ability to know people beyond their appearances, beliefs, and personalities. We perceive the miracle of the love intention behind their incarnation or the dream God has for them. Like watching a stunning sunset, we may even lose ourselves in witnessing their magnificence.

Connecting to and dialoguing with our partner's Soul bypasses all the ego's distractions. We see our partner with crystal clarity, and our relationship takes on an entirely new level of intimacy. We are no longer victims of the ego's masquerade. Our disagreements and resentments are revealed for what they are: side effects of Soulful disconnection. We elevate ourselves above the ego's dramatic story line and gain access to the narrative of Soul.

Ego Talks, Soul Heals

Effective communication is the key to understanding where our partner is coming from. Sometimes, therapy will be essential to disarm hurt feelings and resolve conflicts that are due to miscommunication. But even with professional assistance in effective communication, we may end up understanding only a fraction of each other's reality. If we are not in touch with our Soul essence, we will ask for recognition of our ego's feelings instead of connecting to our more authentic Soul self. This can result in years of unproductive couples therapy, confusion, and lost intimacy.

The strongest motivation of the ego — with all of its complexes, traumas, and neuroses — is to prove its existence and importance. Consciously or unconsciously, pain seeks acknowledgment. Soul shows us this tendency should not be shamed but, rather, met with the grace of love. But Soul also understands that we should not be ignorant or blind. Soul sees with spiritual clarity and refuses to confuse our partner's true self with their egoic suffering. Through the ego-to-their-Soul relationship, we pair healthy communication with intuition. This allows us to pierce through circular and unproductive conversation that is stuck in ego-to-ego relating and instead bring in Soul's higher, and often more efficient, truth (see figure 7).

Ego's crowning objective is to remain intact. Ego strives to win an argument, gain power, or be recognized in its suffering and coddled in martyrdom. The ego does not want to transform; it wants to hold its secure, stubborn position of power. Ego

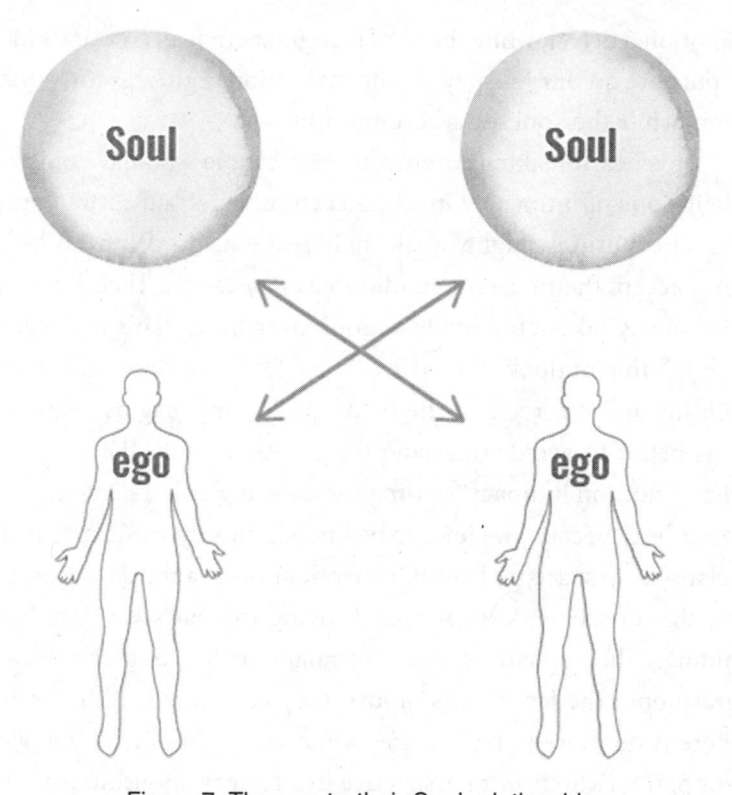

Figure 7. The ego-to-their-Soul relationship

avoids conflict, but when it has to settle its feuds, it likes to use negotiation, bartering, and compromise. It clings to preservation of the status quo in relationship. Ego strives for normalcy and homeostasis, often with insecurity as the driver. Without our re-alizing it, years may go by as we become stuck in stagnant behav-ior and live within rules founded purely from the ego's fear-based reactivity. All too often we resolve the pressing conflicts of the ego but leave the Soul's longing for true intimacy unrequited.

The Soul recognizes the ego's suffering but sees these mo-ments of emotional tension as an opportunity for growth. The ego stays trapped, submersed in the consuming, murky waters of emotional defeat, while the Soul recognizes that all emotions have a purpose on our journey to self-realization. Ego begs for valida-tion, while the Soul seeks communion.

It is heartbreaking when you see a couple who have outlived their hope of intimately meeting each other, afraid certain emo-tional exposures might break their relationship. With no hope, they accept their current condition as a necessity. Their perspec-tive slowly takes on a bitter outlook over time. "This is just how life is," this outlook convinces them. "Relationship is all about settling and not rocking the boat." The couple begins to believe it is better to avoid triggering topics. As a result, they have set their limits on intimacy, settling for knowing only a percentage of the other. (Because we long to be known, this dynamic makes the relationship susceptible to the introduction of a third party, more capable of seeing, knowing, and loving the parts we have been hiding.) The stagnant couple continually convinces themselves to grasp onto the few shards of love they currently hold, believing there is no more to be had. Yet when we begin to dialogue with our partner's Soul, our perspective in all our relationship conflicts changes radically. We soon discover all arguments hold the po-tential to melt our inhibitions toward Divine love.

We had a session with a struggling couple named Ryan and Kate. Their fighting had intensified to a point that made them doubt their relationship would ever work. They had spent years in therapy together with little reward to show for it. We asked them to revisit a fight they had recently had. Our goal was to help them access each other's Souls for insight on what was really going on.

Ryan had made plans to see a friend after work. Kate texted him to come right home after work ended. She was extremely overwhelmed from a day of challenging child-rearing but left this information out of the message. When Ryan received the text, he became angry. He felt his wife was trying to control his evening without even asking if it was OK with him. His offense clashed with her overwhelm, leading to a long and arduous argument.

In our session we asked Ryan to reimagine Kate sending the text — but this time, we directed him to first check in with Kate's Soul. Ryan intuitively asked her Soul what was truly going on with Kate at that moment. Ryan reported, "Her Soul is saying, *Kate is sad. She just really wants me to come home and wrap my arms around her.*" Immediately Ryan's perspective changed. Kate was not trying to undermine Ryan's independence. Kate just felt too vulnerable to ask for what she really wanted: his company and embrace during a difficult time.

We also asked Kate what she would have written to Ryan if she had first connected to his Soul. After centering herself and taking a deep breath, Kate said, "I love you and want you tonight." Needless to say, Ryan's response to this was very different than it had been to her original text.

When we utilize Soul dialoguing with our partner's Soul, our conversations and even our arguments become an entry point for new levels of connection and intimacy. Every action and word directed by Soul shatters unconscious barriers to relationship and facilitates healing. When we keep our conversation within the realm of ego, our love remains egoic, but when we seek guidance from Soul, our love expands into a field of grace.

We can train our ego to listen and reflect our partner's pain, but if we long for a radical unconditional love, we need to go further into Soul expression. Soul's wisdom is unpredictable and may not always fit within a preconceived structure of therapeutic communication. We can know Soul's direction only in and through the present moment. It forces our relationship out of predictability and our routines into the wisdom of the now. It creates a love alive and alluring in all its possibilities.

Besides intimate partnership, Soul connection can be helpful for many different types of life or work relationships. We received an email recently from a client, Gabrielle, who successfully utilized our Soul communication techniques. She works as a Big Sister at an after-school center for kids where there are often conflicts between the adolescents.

> At the after-school club we have three eighth-grade girls who are close friends but have daily friendship drama. One girl always feels left out, and jealousy is a common factor in this threesome.
>
> They came to me very agitated after a recent drama that occurred at a school dance. A mutual crush on a boy created tension, and something happened about how one girl betrayed the other by telling this boy a mildly embarrassing story about her.
>
> In the past, I've always tried to track the details of the drama. But this never goes well, as they always disagree about who said what, who did what to whom, and so on. Instead, I tried what you suggested and asked their Souls what they needed first.
>
> My Soul said, *Jasmine wants to be reflected.* I said something like, "That sounds very hard, Jasmine; I am sorry you had to go through that. I am sure that felt very lonely." She seemed caught off guard and surprised and just became quiet and seemed to calm down a bit.
>
> Next my Soul said, *Let Ella know that she is supported in her friendship.* My ego didn't even understand what was happening in terms of the details of the story, but I said out loud, "Ella, it is normal for friendships to have ups and downs. I know you feel Heather is pulling away. But I know how deeply she cares for you." This seemed to change her emotional state completely. It was like a shift

in the room happened, and everyone went from urgent explaining to a more relaxed state.

The most shocking thing occurred next, when Heather, completely out of character, apologized to the third girl, Ella, for telling this boy something about her homelife. If you knew Heather, you would understand how shocked we all were for this to happen. It is truly some magical stuff, this Soul connecting. It is like their energy knew what I was doing, and it changed the whole vibe of the room. Thank you for teaching me how to do this. I think it will be a game changer!

The power of acknowledging one another on a Soul level offers an undeniable shift in the energetic container of the conversation. This subtle but powerful choice ushers in a spiritual respect, which trickles over to even the most difficult or stubborn egoic conflicts.

Let's Write about It

As we explained in chapter 6, "Hearing Soul's Wisdom," our Soul journaling technique helps build the listening muscle to strengthen the ability to hear specific and practical wisdom from Soul. This technique is not only effective for hearing the voice of your own Soul but also extremely helpful to help you connect to the Souls of others. This practice trains us to become more intuitive with our partners and in all our relationships.

Connecting to the Souls of our fellow workmates is another way Soul journaling can be incredibly useful. You may have heard the statement "People don't quit jobs, they quit bosses." Unfortunately, we frequently hear how toxic work relationships stall career progress. Our client Alex got powerful information through his Soul journaling that enabled him to navigate his micromanaging boss, Dean, at work. Wisdom is the name of Alex's Soul.

> Alex: Why is Dean focusing on my productivity over all the others on my team at work?
>
> Wisdom: *Dean is insecure and plays an alpha role at work, thinking this will win him points with upper management.*
>
> Alex: How do I get off Dean's radar so he stops targeting me?
>
> Wisdom: *It's not about the performance numbers; it's more of an energy he picks up from you. When he senses you are charged, even if you are holding it in, he gets off on that energetic fight.*
>
> Alex: So what do I do?
>
> Wisdom: *Let him know you hear his critique, but then try to get as emotionally neutral as possible so that there is no energy charge for him to fight against. The more you can act disinterested, even though you reflect what he needs to hear, the quicker he will move on to someone else.*

The ego-to-their-Soul relationship can also provide precise Divine direction about how to help our loved ones. This spiritual relationship helps us receive powerful intuitive information far beyond what the ego can fathom. Our next story details the value of connecting beyond ego for practical relationship guidance.

Emma, Wendy and Shaun's four-year-old daughter, had caught a terrible flu. Wendy and Shaun had spent three sleepless nights tending to her. Stress levels were high, spirits were worn down, and both partners were fed up. Wendy felt at the end of her emotional rope. She confessed to us that she had cried on the bathroom floor more than once — which made Shaun's lack of empathy that much more confusing. Wendy described, "When my child is sick, there is nothing more terrible. Every moment with her it feels like my heart is breaking, over and over. I just can't stand to see her suffering. But Shaun, he's fine. I just don't understand it, it's like he has no feelings."

Shaun pleaded to his wife that this was not true. He explained he was just trying to take care of their daughter his own way. Wendy continued in her comments about his "feeling-less" nature, and Shaun began to get agitated back. He told us, "I didn't understand why we had to talk about this now, when our daughter was sick. She was making my job so much harder."

Wendy was no stranger to Soul dialoguing. She knew our work and had been actively journaling for almost a year. So we first turned our attention to Wendy's Soul. Instead of Wendy remaining trapped in her ego's interpretation of Shaun's feelings or lack thereof, Wendy used the ego-to-their-Soul relationship model to ask what was truly going on with Shaun. The information she received was shocking. This is a segment from Wendy's Soul journal:

> Why does Shaun feel disconnected from me?
> *He loves you and Emma; this is not up for debate. He loves you both unconditionally and forever. Imagine the pain you are in. He feels it too; he feels it more.*
> Then why does he feel distant?
> *He is assessing the situation. He needs to know Emma is safe first, and then he will process your emotions.*
> Now that Emma is OK, how can I help Shaun feel?
> *There was a girl who lived by him when he was young, his neighbor.*

Wendy had completely forgotten a memory Shaun had shared with her years ago, but now it came back. His neighbor, a five-year-old girl, had died from pneumonia.

Is this why Shaun is emotionally cut off? Is he worried
    Emma will die?
Yes. Tell his ego what you've learned, and he will feel again.

Wendy brought the Soul conversation to Shaun. He too cried,
but fortunately not on the bathroom floor. He had carried post-
traumatic stress from the death of that dear friend since a young
age. Whenever his own kids got sick, his survivor's guilt was activated. Now, both Wendy and Shaun are consciously aware of his
wound and have embarked on a path of true healing.

Ego versus Soul Relating

When we move beyond egoic communication to Soul communication, we experience an energetic shift in intimacy. We move from
ego relating to Soul relating. Identifying and understanding this
subtle shift on a feeling level helps us proceed to the next plane
of relationship with clarity and certainty. To experience Holy Love
with another, we have to expand our perception. Meeting our own
Soul requires us to become aware of the subtle hunches, instincts,
and guidance of our hearts. To get to know the Soul of another, we
bring awareness to how we intuitively feel in their presence.

Adam Speaks

One summer I trekked up to a small island off the coast of Alaska.
I had landed a job on a fishing boat headed out to the Bering Sea.
It wasn't until after our boat launched that I found out I was re-
placing a man who had been crushed in a crane-loading accident
days before. The sea air around the crew was hung with grief. Yet
mixed with this grief was also a general resentment toward me,
perhaps caused by the sight of a stranger filling the fishing boots
of their lost friend. I became the face that symbolized their loss,
the heartbreak and dangers of the sea.

There was one fisherman, to my utmost gratitude, who showed me only friendship. We shared our meals together morning, noon, and night. Day after day he told me about what he would spend his money on from the job. As the days wore on, the dreams grew bigger. A car turned from a Camry into a Lamborghini, a trip to Hawaii turned into a vacation home. It was as if the longer the crew spent out at sea, the stronger the desperation for dreams became.

About a month in, our boat hit a terrible storm. It was too rough to fish and the potential financial loss too great for us to return to port. So we clung to our seats for three days, waiting for the storm to pass. On the third night, the storm worsened. My newfound friend and I sat at our empty table, too sick to eat, too shaken to sleep.

That night our conversation changed. Without warning, he turned to me and divulged that the man who died had been one of his best friends and he knew, in his heart, his friend would have liked me. He told me that his friend would have accepted me as part of the crew, so he would, too. This whole time I had assumed he knew this man the least out of the crew. He hadn't brought him up once in our many conversations. Now, I understood the opposite was true. It was his deep attachment and respect for his lost friend that inspired his kindness toward me.

Our friendship changed radically that night. I felt as if we had only been acting before, when underneath lived a more sincere friendship. I truly believe that if we had not hit that storm, this secret would have stayed buried under our trivial conversations about fancy cars. But adrenaline, shared camaraderie, and fifty-foot swells had broken this man's barriers to intimacy. He told me about his family, his home in Vietnam, and his two sweet daughters, who tenderly took care of his chickens when he was away. I too shared every detail about my life back home. By the end of the night, we were both laughing, submerged in our memories. The giant waves crashing against the small circular windows were only a backdrop to our Soulful connection. That night our ego-to-ego relationship ended and a new Soulful one began. Before we hadn't really known each other, and now he felt like family.

When we move from ego relating to Soul relating, it feels like a tension is released that we previously didn't even know was there. Authentic Soul connection moves us and changes us. Our conversations and interactions leave us feeling full and alive. Soul connection awakens a deeper love from its slumber in our hearts. That night Adam peeled back only one layer of ego within his friendship with his crewmate. The depths we dive into with each other are endless once we begin to follow the path of Soul relating.

All our relationships are an interweaving of both ego and Soul relating. But with clear intention, we can consciously cultivate Soul relating in almost any relationship. Although it can be challenging to reach out to another's Soul when ego presses for our attention, the rewards are worth it. If we can be disciplined, remembering to consistently orient to the Soul of our partner during conflict, we are rewarded with an opportunity to evolve our relationship to a truly spiritual level. Our determined focus exposes the infinite goodness of our partner's Soul, creating the atmosphere to alchemize the relationship from an egoic one into one that is eternal and Soul connected. Through the ego-to-their-Soul relationship, we discover the magnificence of our partner's unique nature. The process of understanding each other becomes a never-ending, miraculous journey. Every step we take toward their true nature increases our compassion and love for them. No longer is the person standing in front of us a limited and defined personality; they are an endless universe to admire. When we use the ego-to-their-Soul relationship, we can no longer deny another's Divine nature. We begin to see and feel glimpses of Soul through the other person. This is where the real miracle of sacred relating begins.

THEIR SOUL NATURE INQUIRY

Use the questionnaire below to help you identify what you already know and appreciate about the Soul of a loved one. You can use this exercise with your partner or anyone you know on a deep personal level. Don't overthink your answers; we will go more into seeing and feeling the Soul in the following chapters.

A helpful variation of this exercise is to answer the questions twice: first taking your ego's best guess and then taking your Soul's perspective through journaling. The differences can be surprising.

- Try to describe the Soul of the person in question. What makes this person entirely unique?
- What does their Soul *feel* like to you? Use feeling quality descriptions like the ones in the feeling chart on page 100.
- What does their Soul value?
- What does their Soul enjoy or love to do?
- What is an activity you can do together that would fulfill their Soul?
- Are there any words or actions you could employ that would show recognition for their Soul?

THE HEAD VERSUS THE HEART

Identifying our own egoic versus Soulful emotions, thoughts, and actions is a useful step toward embodying Soul. Egoic emotions are from our minds. They often come from a perspective of feeling offended or betrayed by certain values or from a need for validation. Soul emotions most often come from the heart, arising spontaneously and generously. You can glance at the lists of ego versus Soul qualities in the table below as a refresh. Then, brainstorm and write down on figure 8 whatever resonates from the lists or first pops into your head about how you feel and act when coming from the ego (head) versus the Soul (heart). No editing!

EGO VERSUS SOUL QUALITIES

EGO	SOUL
Mind	Heart
Fear based	Love based
Focused on the past or future	In the present
Material, mortal, temporary, physical	Spiritual, eternal
Identifying as personality or persona (roles)	Identifying as Soul essence (multidimensional or energetic awareness)
Separation	Connection
What I am getting or doing	What I am becoming or being
Life feels meaningless	Life feels meaningful
Rules and morality for guidance	Inner unique guidance
External power (power over)	Internal power (power within)
Control, doubt, manipulation, and game playing	Authentic vulnerability, trust
Reactive and dramatic	Centered and grounded
Selfish, withholding, taking	Seeking the highest good of all Souls involved, generous
Needing approval, judgmental	Connected to purpose, Soul orchestration, and contracts
Feeling never enough, comparing self to others	Fulfilled and complete

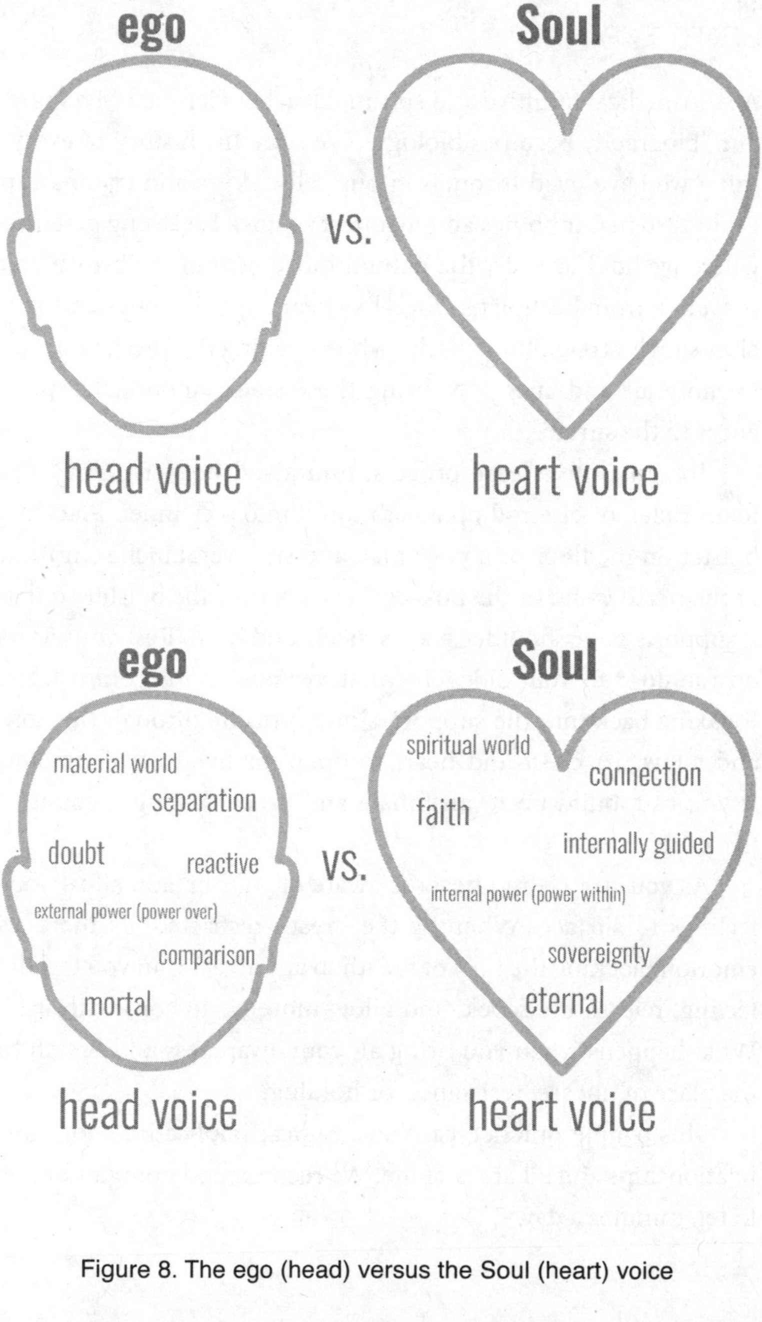

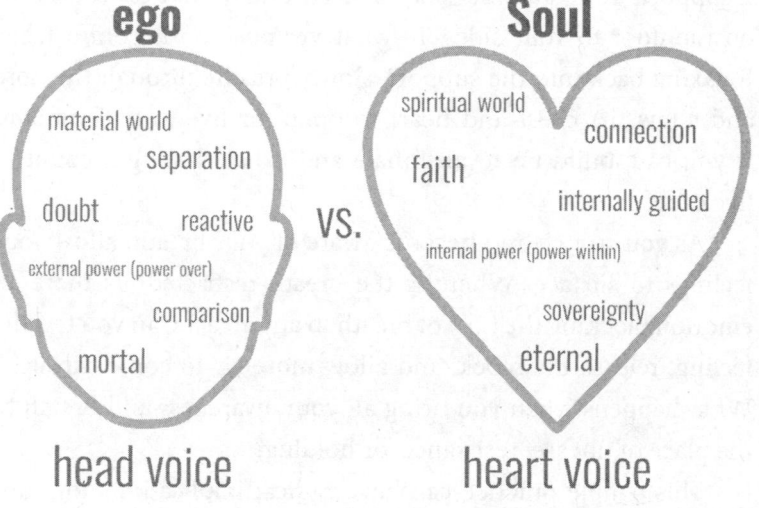

Figure 8. The ego (head) versus the Soul (heart) voice

HEART EXPANSION

As the medical intuitive and spiritual teacher Caroline Myss says, our "biography becomes biology." We store the history of everything we have lived through in our cells. Stress and trauma can get lodged in our bodies and manifest as stuck breathing patterns, where we hold or resist the natural movement of the breath and prevent it from healing us. Yoga-like heart-opening physical exercises slowly stretch the muscles while opening the chest, allowing in more air and energy to bring these stuck emotional experiences to the surface.

To assist the release process, find a soft bolster pillow or a foam roller, or else roll up a bath towel into a cylinder. Place the bolster on the floor or a yoga mat, and sit several inches in front of the narrow end of the bolster. Lie back over the bolster so that it supports your shoulder blades, neck, and head. Rest your arms on the floor to your sides, in whatever position is comfortable. Relaxing back into the support, slowly breathe through the nose and allow the chest and heart to open for five to ten minutes. If you can, build up to an inhale and exhale lasting a count of five each.

As you stretch and become aware of your breath, allow your feelings to surface. Where is the breath restricted? Is there an emotion blocking the flow of breath to any areas? Can you feel the feeling, release the block, and allow more air to come through? What happens when you bring all your awareness and breath to the place of unease, resistance, or holding?

This simple practice can have radical implications for your relationships and all areas of life. We recommend doing it for five to ten minutes a day.

MEDITATION: MEET THEIR SOUL

An audio version of this meditation is available for free online at holyandhuman.com/holylove.

We will spend the following meditation getting to know the Soul of another person. Getting to know another's Soul is similar to praying for someone we love. They do not need to be in the same physical location to receive the prayer, as it is the love itself that creates the energetic connection. If you do not have good intentions toward or a loving relationship with this person, the meditation will not work.

Find a peaceful place where you will not be disturbed or interrupted. Sit up comfortably with your feet on the floor. Do not cross your arms or legs.

We will begin this meditation with box breathing, which has four parts. Sitting upright, exhale the air out of your lungs. Now inhale through your nose and slowly count to four in your mind. Feel the air expanding your lungs until they are completely full. Now hold your breath while slowly counting to four again. Exhale through your mouth and count to four as you feel the air expelling from your lungs and abdomen. After the exhale, again hold your breath until you have slowly counted to four in your mind. Repeat by inhaling through your nose and counting to four. Hold the breath in for four. Release the breath through your mouth for four and hold the breath out for four. Take the next few moments to find a natural rhythm with this cycle. If you like, you can imagine blowing all anxiety and worries out on the exhale and imagine receiving peace, goodness, and relaxation on the inhale.

Now return to breathing naturally, without holding the breath in or out. We will now use active imagination to connect first with our own Soul. Do not overthink the following instructions but rather see if you can allow or receive the answer. Take a natural breath. Now ask your Soul what color it would like to be represented as. Once you have picked a color, imagine it filling your heart entirely with love. Place a hand on your heart and spend a moment feeling into the energy of your Soul. See if you can acknowledge or become reacquainted with this essence that makes you unique. In your mind, ask if Soul, the color in your heart, has a message for you before you continue.

Now, bring your focus back to your breath. Allow it to flow naturally. Bring the name of the person you would like to connect with into your mind. Set the intention to feel and see the miracle of their higher self, their love nature. Ask your Soul to choose a color (or colors) to represent their Soul. Make sure this is a different color from the one you have chosen to represent your own Soul. Once you have picked a color, bring your awareness to how this color feels. How does it feel different than your Soul? See if you can find a few words to describe the unique characteristics of this color. For example, does the color feel strong, confident, or perhaps playful and graceful? Notice if there are any correlating characteristics between this Soul and the person you've chosen to connect with. If the answer is yes, this is a sign you are now in dialogue with their Soul.

When you are ready, ask their Soul a question in your mind. Allow yourself to receive the answer. You can ask multiple questions and respond to their answers, just like in a normal conversation. Feel free to continue the dialogue for as long as feels right.

If you are having difficulties, remind yourself that this is a skill and takes practice like any other skill. You can always try again. If you are having doubts about the information you are receiving, discuss it with your chosen person afterward. This is a great way to validate correct information and identify information that is off.

When you are ready, say goodbye to the color of the other person's Soul. Imagine sending the color back to the person you have chosen, with love. And bring your attention back to your own color. If you still see or feel any residual color from the other Soul, just take another moment to imagine it flowing back to the chosen person.

Now imagine your own Soul color expanding from the center of your heart. Imagine it filling up your chest, torso, arms, hands, and fingers. Imagine it flowing down your legs to your feet. Now see it flowing up your neck and into your face and head. Breathe and feel this color throughout you as your unique version of love.

When you are ready, open your eyes.

CHAPTER 10

Seeing the Soul

The summary of the advice of all prophets is this:
Find yourself a mirror.

— Shams Tabrizi

Now that we have learned how to hear another's Soul and feel ego-to-their-Soul relating, we will focus on how to *see* the Soul. When we use the ego-to-their-Soul relationship, our perception of our loved ones radically shifts. We start to view them through the multidimensional awareness of Soul rather than the funneled-down rational interpretation of ego. In Hinduism, this state of seeing is called Satcitananda.

During Adam's stay in India, his multiple host families and newfound friends struggled to pronounce his American name. With the Hindi accent it came out sounding more like "Arum." So when his host father bestowed on him the nickname "Anand," it stuck for the rest of the year. *Anand* in Sanskrit means "happiness, ecstatic joy, and sensual pleasure." *Satcitananda* is compounded from three Sanskrit words, including this formidable nickname.

Sat means "real or true existence"; *cit* is "to perceive, comprehend, or know"; and we are already familiar with *ananda*. Satcitananda, then, is to perceive the true beauty of existence through the senses.

Seeing with love allows us to enter a state of gratitude, drop into the moment, and perceive the real beauty in front of our very eyes. This change in perception may be difficult for a Western mind to wrap itself around, but we can all understand it via the age-old concept of love at first sight. No matter how many years have passed since our first meeting, we can continue to see our partners through the experience of love at first sight. This is, in fact, one of our most natural states of being. Comparison, judgment, and criticism are what block our vision from seeing Soul in one another. Finding Soul's vision of love is not a new skill — it is the most natural one we've ever known. We only need to defog our mental glasses and witness from the heart.

The widely revered spiritual teacher and author Adyashanti explains, "Awakening happens when you stop bullshitting yourself into continual nonawakening." In other words, because "being awake" is our natural state, we don't have to *do anything in particular* to awaken; we just need to stop bullshitting ourselves — and then *we are* awakened. The same is true for seeing the Soul in others: in the absence of fogged glasses, we naturally see the glorious Soul standing right before us, and we are naturally in love. This chapter teaches how to clean off our lenses so we can be in that natural state.

We cannot see the Soul if we value only the physical, but this does not mean that Soul doesn't value and inhabit the physical. Many people interpret spiritual perception as the ability to see past or feel nonattached to the physical human form. But if only the spiritual is valued and the physical is dismissed, we live detached from an essential part of our nature. William Blake wrote, "Man has no body distinct from his Soul; for that called Body is a portion of a Soul discerned by the five Senses." It bears repeating; we do not possess a body that is separate from the Soul. Nor, as the common conception seems to be, are we merely a physical body with a Soul dwelling somewhere inside or above us. Rather, we are bodies imbued with Soul. Soul resides in every cell. We see hints and reflections of the Soul in the physical form. Soul seeps through our voice, our gestures, even the way we sleep. It is these physical signatures and Soul idiosyncrasies we end up cherishing most in our loved ones. Over time, the subtle yet intricate physical connection between us and another begins to feel familiar and helps us identify their Soul nature.

It is easy to believe we are just making up the concept of Soul, yet Soul is quite literally making you up. Soul is your unique energetic signature, creating and animating each and every single cell. The body is an extension, or an expression, of the all-encompassing Soul; it is Soul made manifest in form. Our uniquely beautiful body, movements, and mannerisms are all microcosms of the expansive macrocosm of Soul.

Our client Camille has been married for eleven years and came to us out of curiosity. After our session, we sent Camille home with some guided exercises (included at the end of this chapter), and she returned to the next session exuberant. She described her experience in Soul witnessing with her partner:

> We were lying in bed. I was disappointed because I wasn't seeing anything out of the ordinary. I felt stupid even trying, like I was pretending to be spiritual. I felt like a poser. But then I remembered to see with my love for him. I focused on my love for him, and immediately everything changed. Actually, nothing changed, it all looked exactly the same. But a *quality* changed in the room, like everything had more depth and light in it. And when I saw him, I fell in love all over again.

When we witness another's Soul, we are filled with meaning and reverence. In this witnessing, we see with our hearts and are forever changed by the beauty before us. With our intuitive sense, we feel a gravitation and high-level attraction toward certain people: we recognize their beauty perhaps more than anyone else does. In our true Soul desire and intuitive gaze, they appear physically irresistible. This is because Soul's love and the physical no longer exist in separate compartmentalized realms. Holy Love brings a lust for every inch of our lovers. In long-term relationships, if we are able to see true beauty in each other, our original desire is revitalized. When we search, not for physical beauty, but for Soul beauty, we begin to see the beauty that lives through us. Only then can we notice the magnificence in her hands, the mysterious depths in his eyes, or the hidden constellations in the freckles down her back.

Those with the eyes of Soul understand profound beauty through the physical, regardless of form. They see that beauty does not leave our partners when they get cancer, with their shaved heads and feeble bodies, or when they grow a gut, sprout hair in their ears, and get wrinkles down their neck. Soul is not stuck in the past, longing for the good old days when we were young and conventionally attractive; Holy Love longs for the love embrace in each and every age and stage. Beauty is in the eye of the beholder, and when we are seen on a Soul level, we are beheld in our true beauty.

When we connect to another's Soul, we are simply drawn to the inherent energy in the other. Through the eyes of Soul, our partner's beauty permeates the room, ignites our hearts, and inspires our devotion. Our desire does not fade over time but grows. We do not need to sexually entertain ego in order to turn Soul on. As Soul lovers, we are not tethered to the mainstream myth that long-term desire is maintained solely by making an effort to connect to our partner through costumes, fantasies, and sexual gymnastics. The eyes of Soul see through all states of humanity and humility to the Divinity that stirs underneath performance and presentation. Soul understands the true meaning of unconditional love, beyond the physical conditions of the body.

Egoic desire clings to physical form, while Soul desire longs for eternal union. Ego desire sees the body only for its appeal and wants it selfishly, like a well-presented meal. Soul desire seeks spiritual connection and eternal ravishment. Soul wants the seen and the unseen, the physical and the spiritual, the earth and the heavens. While ego is turned on by the culturally sought-after ideal of physical beauty, Soul is turned on by love.

When retreat participants list the reasons why they love their partners, often their first answer feels superficial and generic. They may answer, "She is so kind and funny" or "He always takes care of me." If we reframe the question as "If your partner passed away, what would you miss about them?" the answers become much more specific, personalized, and heartfelt. One participant said, "I would miss the way she holds my hand when we watch a movie. She puts her hand right on top of my open palm." Another answered, "I would miss how he always kisses my eyelids after sex." And one participant simply said, "I would miss watching him read." Most of us are currently unaware of the value these moments have in our relationships. We may not miss the way he holds his coffee cup or the way she smiles until we are away from our partners or they have left us. In either case, whether we are aware or unaware, these moments are the ones we hold on to, the ones that make them uniquely *them*. When we remember these, they clear away egoic debris and remind us of the other's essence.

In modern relationships, it is common to blind ourselves to Soul. How often do we overlook the slight pain on our partner's face because we are running on autopilot? How often do we miss

the miracle of the child before us because we are frustrated with
the mess they created? We fall into roles, tasks, and imaginary
time lines for each other and ourselves, completely missing the
alive and present exchange that is always available to us in each
moment.

The mind, and language in particular, can cause us to be oblivious to the spiritual world unfolding before us. During his life, the
spiritual teacher Krishnamurti often lectured and wrote about the
limitations of the mind created by the labeling of language. He
believed our spiritual task was to continue to stay awake from the
hypnotic spell of interpretation and live in the present moment
with the world. In his book *Freedom from the Known* he wrote:
"Do you know that even when you look at a tree and say, 'That is
an oak tree'... the naming of the tree, which is botanical knowledge, has so conditioned your mind that the word comes between
you and actually seeing the tree? To come in contact with the tree
you have to put your hand on it and the word will not help you to
touch it." Our spiritual task is to stay in the present moment while
seeing and experiencing the Soul purely and directly. Even the
most mundane tasks, in the eyes of a loving beholder, will seem
full of an angel's grace — how she brushes her teeth or the way
he checks the rearview mirror. A parent may see the Soul of their
child in the way they tie their shoes, color a drawing, or quietly
sing to themselves. Even when we are angry at our partners or
have resentments from the past, if Soul vision is activated, we can
be shocked by the beauty and attraction we experience toward
our partner's essence. These moments begin to become evidence
for the presence of the Soul behind all action.

It is the act of witnessing and loving simultaneously that allows us to see beyond and through the physical form. In other
words, the more we love someone, the more we recognize these
Soul moments. And the more distant and detached we become,

the less we recognize their phenomenal beauty. The miracle of how he shaves is seen only through how she loves him. There is no egoic interpretation that finds the way she snores endearing; the sweet quality of her snore is known only by a true witness of her unique beauty.

A birth seen through the empty eyes of literalism potentially looks repugnant. Seen through love, it is pure miracle. To most people, life is nonsensical, because they remain trapped in a world of purely material observance. Yet if we witness with love, we witness the Soul. In the words of Ralph Waldo Emerson: "It takes a poet to truly see the stars." Through the heart, our literal senses and our love may enter a consubstantial state. The physical and the holy merge before our eyes.

If this seems unattainable, just notice how you feel the next time you find yourself caught in one of those stolen moments with someone you love. We tend to revel in these moments but also quickly dismiss them and return to our habituated patterns of thought. Next time, stop and marinate in the feeling that arises. We must teach ourselves to *notice* once again. You may be pleasantly surprised. Time slows, and the world around you feels as if it shifts into vivid Technicolor. Nothing else matters. The moment feels perfect, but not by any definition of perfection you have known previously. Life is complete. You are stunned by the magnitude of the eternal as your heart blooms into expansiveness. This is the joy that comes from witnessing Soul in another person. True love opens the door to profound spiritual experience that most of us are just too busy or distracted to notice.

Projection

To meet another person on a Soul level, we need to be aware of where we are blocking ourselves from this union. By far the most common cause of Soul blindness in relationships is a defense mechanism in our psyche called projection. Projection is a form of distortion in our perception of others. A projection occurs when we disown a feeling or belief we would rather not face or accept in ourselves. We then incorrectly attribute the disavowed feeling to another person. Because we cannot access the feeling internally, we project it out, externally. Just like a movie projector in a theater, the subconscious outputs an image (from past experiences or beliefs) onto another person. We can see only the movie from our past and are blinded to the true nature of our partner before us. For instance, if we have experienced a betrayal of trust in a previous relationship, we may project that experience onto a current partner and have trouble trusting the relationship we are in. In essence, we mistakenly see the past cheating boyfriend or girlfriend instead of the current loyal one before us.

Projections invariably block Soul intimacy. Gaining insight to our projections greatly speeds up the process of Soul relating and cultivates self-discovery. Each time we recognize a psychological projection, we have an opportunity to become more conscious and reclaim a lost part of ourselves. Projections are not to be judged as "bad." For humans, projecting to some degree is inevitable. Most marriages start with many projections, and over time, we release the false version of our partner and are able to meet, accept, and love the person we have actually married.

A true story from Tibet serves as a perfect parable for projection. In 1955 a group of monks in Thailand were tasked with moving a giant clay statue of the Buddha. As they tried to hoist the statue's massive weight, the ropes tied to it broke. The Buddha fell and cracked. But what seemed to be a disaster was soon revealed to be a miracle. One of the monks noticed golden light emanating through the broken clay shell. Underneath layers of clay was a solid gold statue. Historians dated the clay layers to be two hundred years old. They believe that in an attempt to protect the golden statue from an invading Burmese army, a group of Buddhists concealed its original state, and the statue's secret was lost to time.

We may not be facing an invading army, but we do face our own inner battles. Through projection, our unconscious beliefs create layers of mud over others, concealing the true nature of their identity. Whether the qualities being projected are desirable or undesirable, wanted or unwanted, positive or negative, the result is the same: they all cause alienation. As long as major projections live in our relationship, we cannot achieve honest intimacy, because we are stuck in a neurotic relationship with ourselves. We form an idol of our partner and choose to see what we want to see in them. But when we remove projections, we stop chasing fool's gold and begin the search for the true gold of the Soul.

Projections generally fall into one of two categories: positive projections and negative projections. A positive projection happens when we see in another a positive trait that we have not allowed ourselves to claim. It is common to project onto celebrities, teachers, or leaders. We may project our own beauty onto the dancer on stage, assuming this expression of grace is reserved for others and not inherent within us. We may project creativity onto our favorite musician, worshipping their songs while leaving our own potential in hibernation. Or we may see greatness in our business tycoons and other figures with power, unaware of our own untapped reservoir of empowerment. Where we worship kindness, daring, or talent in another, we may be waiting to claim our own.

On the other end of the spectrum, a negative projection occurs when we disown an unpleasant feeling or belief about our self and instead see it in another. Negative projections hide in the shadowy realm of jealousies, hurt feelings, and arguments. This is a common source of endless conflict in relationships as we become players in the blame game. Both partners deny their part, disowning their inherent insecurity and escalating the fight. After the argument, both play the conversation back in their heads, rewriting the narrative in their favor, continuing their negative projections.

These false perceptions do great damage. A subconscious belief that we are unlovable may suddenly convince us that our partner actually does not love us. We may interpret the simplest action, like our partner going out with friends, as a personal betrayal. The insecure projection can be extremely convincing: "She doesn't enjoy my company." Another common negative projection is that of cheating. If one partner has considered cheating but disowned the thought, they may live in constant suspicion of the other partner's desire to cheat (whether the partner actually has that desire or not). This serves to displace their own guilt and distracts them from dealing with their own emotions. That is why it is common for someone who has been unfaithful to become extremely possessive toward their partner.

Projections can also take hold within a collective. For example, because of the intense cultural, and often religious, stigma against homosexuality, internalized homophobia can cause a religious man to judge other homosexuals when he is struggling with his own homosexual attractions. In these cases the muddy layers no longer resemble a Buddha but a monster. When we project onto others, we end up treating them in ways that reflect how we unconsciously feel about ourselves. We fight an invisible enemy of our own self-acceptance. We become like the delusional knight Don Quixote, fighting imaginary windmills that we have projected our own giants onto.

But projections can also be beneficial. When worked with consciously, projections can invite a deeper understanding of others and ourselves. Positive projections serve as bridges over chasms; our teachers, heroes, and idols can inspire us to find greater qualities in ourselves. Negative projections serve as mirrors, showing us through another person what we might be holding in the shadows.

Projections, though very real, are also flimsy. When challenged with Soul truth, their illusory power immediately vanishes. Using the ego-to-their-Soul relationship model is the most efficient way to expose projections within a relationship. When caught in projection, we function from distorted information, leading to distorted relationships. As we examine and remove our projections from our partners, we become available for true Soul communion. Soul's information adjusts the mind to a new, clear reality and opens our eyes to the unique, honest beauty of the people we love.

SEEING THE ENERGY OF THE SOUL

Saints are often depicted in medieval and Renaissance paintings wearing golden, radiant halos. Those spiritual avatars incarnated such a high wattage of Divine Soul energy that their auras could be seen and recorded even by an energetically untrained eye. The rest of us may not be radiating at such a high wattage, but we all have Soul, and we all carry a spiritual glow — it may just need the assistance of intuitive perception to be seen.

In fact, the body emits Soul's illumination, like a light bulb. We need only look through the eyes of our Soul to perceive Soul's light in another and to feel its warmth, as the following exercise shows. It should be done with a partner in a dimly lit room; make sure there are no lights behind either of you. Both partners should follow the steps simultaneously. You can also practice it by yourself in a mirror.

1. Sit across from each other in a comfortable position. It
    will be easier to see Soul energy if each person is posi-
    tioned in front of a blank wall (ideally one that is a light
    gray). If you don't have a blank wall, choose backgrounds
    that don't have too many bright colors or objects. Just like
    in a painting, the colors will pop more on a blank surface
    than on one that is busy.

2. Both participants close their eyes, take a few deep breaths,
    and relax.

3. With your eyes still closed, bring your attention to how
    you *feel* in the other person's presence. This will open
    your intuitive senses.

4. Set the intention to see their Soul by repeating these three
    phrases in your mind: "I am ready to see the Soul in front
    of me. I am willing to see the Soul in front of me. I will see
    their Soul." If you are a person who is more feeling ori-
    ented than visual, you may notice a sensation of physical
    warmth or emotions surfacing.

5. Open your eyes and maintain eye contact. Allow your
    eyes to relax. It is easiest to see auras with your peripheral
    vision. Without breaking eye contact, see if you notice a
    haze or translucent bubble around the other person. This
    bubble may have color to it. It may fade or increase in in-
    tensity. This is because auras — Soul energy — change on
    the basis of our moods and thoughts. You may also find
    that when you bring your attention to it, it disappears
    completely. This is normal. Take another breath, reestab-
    lish eye contact, and try again.

6. Once you feel comfortable seeing each other's auras,
    begin to experiment. Have your partner sway slightly
    from side to side. See if the energy follows them, like mo-
    lasses. Experiment with this for as long as you like. You

can also look at your hands, between the fingers, to see your own energy.

7. When you are ready to end the exercise, wiggle your toes and your fingertips to bring awareness back to your physical body. Next, slowly stretch out your arms and legs. Through moving your body, you are shifting brain states. Give yourself plenty of time before standing up, as you may feel light-headed or spacey. While you adjust to waking consciousness, share your experience with your partner.

EYE GAZING WITH A PARTNER

The eyes truly are the window to the Soul. When we allow ourselves to see behind appearances, the Soul reveals itself. In her book *Meet Your Soul*, Elisa discussed how to do the practice of eye gazing by yourself. Now we will focus this powerful practice on a partner. Both partners should follow the steps simultaneously. The practice seems simple, but don't underestimate its potency.

1. Sit about two to three feet across from someone with whom you feel emotionally safe. You can be seated in chairs or on the floor. Close your eyes and take at least ten deep breaths to begin to relax and adjust your brain states.

2. With your eyes closed, set the intention to see their Soul. In your head or out loud, state, "I am ready to meet your Soul. Thank you for revealing your self."

3. Now open your eyes. As you hold each other's gaze, allow yourself to receive the Soul of the other. Without reaching out or seeking, allow yourself to receive a feeling, impression, or visual of the other's Soul. At first, resistance or

discomfort often arises at the emotional intimacy of this exercise. You may feel self-conscious or want to laugh or cry. Allow any emotion to arise and let it out, without judgment. Let the wave of discomfort be expressed and released.

4. Remember, everyone receives intuitive information in different ways. Visuals often present themselves: the face before you may morph into another, a totem animal may appear, or some may even witness the individual progressively age right in front of them. The Soul is speaking through images and revealing a story. Although it can be startling to the ego, continue to breathe if you experience any powerful visuals.

   Others receive intuitive information through emotion; they may be deeply moved by the practice or overwhelmed by a feeling of love and familiarity. If strong feelings arise, continue to breathe and stay present. Some people receive downloads of knowing or past-life memories of the Soul connection. Again, continue to breathe. Do not put expectations on the process or force any one particular thing to happen. Just breathe and stay present with whatever the moment wants to show you.

5. Continue the practice for about five to ten minutes. If at the end of the practice you do not feel much has occurred, know you are warming up the ego to the practice. You may need another round, or several, to build safety and allow the ego to adjust to the spiritual experience. Try to avoid becoming frustrated and just continue to revisit the exercise with an open mind and heart. Often, energetic shifts are occurring even when flashy visuals are absent. Congratulate yourself each time you prioritize these Soul encounters.

WITHDRAWING PROJECTIONS

As we've discussed, when we project our unconscious material onto another, we cannot meet them in authentic intimacy. The following exercise can help us make our unconscious projections conscious, own them, and withdraw them from the other person. This practice is meant to be done alone. Have paper and pen or your computer handy.

1. **Identify.** Identify someone toward whom you have a strong emotional charge. It can be someone you have been ruminating on or an individual who brings up strong emotions when you think of them. Bring them to mind, but before you allow the emotion to overcome you, take a moment to breathe and relax.

2. **List three of the person's triggering qualities.** Write down three qualities that describe that person and bring up strong emotion when you think of them. For example: "Judy is inconsiderate, brash, and direct."

3. **Write down how you feel in this person's presence.** For example: "When I am around Judy, I feel unvalued, nervous, disrespected."

4. **Seek your feeling's origins.** Spend some time reflecting on the feelings you wrote down. Trace your own history around the qualities that trigger you and the feelings they engender. What are their possible origins — perhaps family experiences, a formative event, or a past relationship? For example: "Judy reminds me of my Aunt Sandy, who never acknowledged my feelings. Sandy is also brash and seeks attention. I feel in similar ways around Judy as I do around Sandy."

5. **Put yourself in the other person's shoes.** When we project, we simplify other people's emotions and dehumanize

their actions. Start to withdraw the projection by flipping it around: ask yourself what might be going on with you if you were acting out with those same qualities. For example: "When I myself act rude, it is because I feel isolated, fearful, and sad." Then ask yourself if it is possible you are misinterpreting their motives or feelings. If the answer is yes, allow yourself time to reflect on or Soul journal about why you may have assumed incorrectly.

6. **Grow compassion.** Next, look at where you carry the other person's qualities inside yourself. For example: "Where and in what ways am I rude to others? What circumstances would need to be happening for me to act out in a rude way?" Then, put yourself in the other person's shoes: "Can I find compassion for Judy when I realize she must be feeling that way much of the time?"

7. **Reflect.** You will know when you finish withdrawing a projection because the emotional charge will shift. Instead of being focused externally on the other person's actions, your focus will be internal, on your own psychological discoveries. Crying is common in the withdrawal of both positive and negative projections as we reclaim parts of ourselves we have previously disowned. For positive projections, we welcome back our light; with negative projections, we become closer to our shadow, increasing love and compassion for others as well as ourselves.

8. **Lastly, journal about your discoveries.** Did you gain any insight? What was it? Did your compassion increase? Could you forgive yourself or another? What dots were you able to connect on the topic? Are there any missing pieces that still need to be reclaimed? How will life be different now that this projection is withdrawn? The more we heal, the less charge the other person has in our lives,

and the more we see them with objectivity and compassion. But make no mistake: removing a projection can be intense. The process often brings up strong emotions we've been avoiding. Have compassion for yourself and for the person you've projected onto. Projection is a human experience we all go through. By withdrawing a projection from someone else, you have taken responsibility for your contribution to a difficult relationship or conflict. This is a major step to creating honest and loving connection in all of your relationships.

BEYOND THE LABEL

When we label people or things into categories, they lose their life force and power to touch us. In the spirit of Krishnamurti, this exercise will increase your ability to see and experience the world directly, without limiting your understanding through the narrow lens of labeling. The practice increases our sensitivity so we can see with all of our awareness, not only our eyes.

If you are doing this exercise outdoors, find a beautiful tree or bush covered in flowers where you feel safe to sit and relax. If indoors, sit by a plant, animal, crystal, or candle. Begin by placing a hand on your heart to bring you into your body and slow down racing thoughts.

Now, rest your gaze on the flowering bush, candle, or other object you are next to. In light meditation, practice staying open and present in exchange with the presence or energy of the plant or object in the current moment. Try to do this for three to ten minutes. You may need to start with a short period and work up to greater times.

Once you feel comfortable with this exercise, take it into the world and practice expanding your gaze with other people. You could start by noticing the child on the bus, your aunt across the kitchen, or your partner while they are doing dishes. Try to stay in the present and really see and feel them as their energy. Over time, as you continue to practice, you will find that it feels increasingly natural to be truly in the moment with yourself and others.

MEDITATION: SEEING THE SOUL

An audio version of this meditation is available for free online at holyandhuman.com/holylove.

> Find a peaceful place to be with your partner where you will not be disturbed or interrupted, ideally a room that is not too brightly lit. Choose a comfortable position sitting across from each other.

> Close your eyes. Bring your awareness to your breath. Simply notice the sensation of your inhale and exhale. Let your system slow down from the pace of your day until you feel your breath coming and going in a natural rhythm.

> After your next exhale, take a long, slow breath in through your nose. Direct the air into your lower lungs or stomach. Hold your breath in for the count of three. And then slowly release it through your mouth. As you exhale, imagine your body releasing any stress. Slowly inhale once more through the nose, hold for three, and slowly exhale when you are ready, letting go of any tension. Take a moment to repeat these steps at your own natural pace.

> As you breathe, allow your breath to naturally deepen and slow down. On your inhale, remember to pull the air into your stomach. If it's comfortable to do so, you can slow down the

pace of your count as you hold your breath. Each time you exhale, imagine your body becoming even more relaxed.

Now, return to normal breathing, without holding on the inhale. Keeping your eyes closed, we will now set the intention of our meditation. Repeat these three phrases in your head: "I am ready to meet the Soul in front of me. I am willing to see the Soul in front of me. I will know their Soul."

Still keeping your eyes closed, know that you and your partner are going to pretend you have just met each other for the very first time. Allow yourself to temporarily erase from your mind all the personal history you have together. When you open your eyes, instead of noticing each other's physical features, you will bring your awareness to each other's essence. You will try to imagine, if you were meeting this person for the first time, what their essence would *feel* like to you.

You may now open your eyes, but remain silent. Remember, the person sitting in front of you is a Soul incarnated in a body. In this present moment, they do not have any words or actions that define them. Try to identify what it is that *does* define them in this moment. What is it that makes them one of a kind? Do not answer this question from past experiences but from what you notice in this present moment. Allow yourself to sit with these questions in silence together.

Now close your eyes again. Bring your attention back to your breath. Find a natural and relaxed pace. Place a hand over your heart. Bring your awareness to the center of your heart. Now see if you can feel your own unique essence. See if you can feel the energy of you. Take another breath and then repeat this phrase in your head: "I am ready to show my Soul. I am willing to show my Soul. I will be my Soul." Imagine a color to represent your Soul. You can choose any color, but pick one that represents your unique version of love. Imagine the color as the *feeling* you just experienced, the energy of you. Imagine this color, or essence, expanding from the center of your heart out into your chest. Imagine the color flowing down your arms and into your fingertips. Now, see it going down your torso, stomach, hips, and legs, all the way into your feet. And imagine the color flowing up your shoulders, neck, face, and head. Repeat this phrase: "I am ready to show my Soul. I am willing to show my Soul. I will be my Soul." Open your eyes.

Notice if you see anything different in your partner. Is their Soul stronger, more apparent, or bolder? If you see no visual difference, focus on what they *feel* like to you. Where is the essence that makes them who they are in this very moment? Look into their eyes and see if you can *feel* the consciousness behind them — their unique internal and eternal self.

Close your eyes once more. Bring your awareness back to your breath. Now we will focus on the true reason we love our partner. Try to remember a happy memory of you together. Don't think about what happened or what you were doing; rather, remember how you felt together. You may recollect a few memories, but focus on the energy of the other's presence. Can you remember *feeling* their essence in these moments? Can you remember their Soul in these memories? After a few moments, recollect feeling love for each other. Remember a time you felt in love. See if you can identify their Soul essence and your own. Marinate in this feeling.

Now open your eyes. Notice what you see and feel. Does their Soul feel even more vivid and awake? Can you *feel* the true identity of your partner? Allow yourself to sit and receive each other's Soul.

When you are ready, share with your partner what you experienced. In meditation we enter an altered state of consciousness, so we may forget what we felt in a few moments, not unlike waking from a dream. In addition to sharing with your partner, now would be a good time to take any notes, so you can review them later. You can also revisit these notes the next time you feel distant or disconnected from each other.

CHAPTER 11

The Soul-to-Soul
Relationship

Love is the most powerful
and still the most unknown energy in the world.

— PIERRE TEILHARD DE CHARDIN

In every relationship, Soul meaning hides camouflaged, waiting for rediscovery of the original dream inherent in the connection between two people. Now that we can intuitively perceive the Soul of another (the ego-to-their-Soul relationship), we will deepen our understanding of the original love intention behind the connection through the Soul-to-Soul relationship. Soul-to-Soul relationships are recognized and honored when we consciously connect to the Soul lessons and contracts that bind us together. Doing this immediately clarifies *why* a particular individual is in your life. When we understand our Soul-to-Soul connection, we discover the map of the terrain from our heart to their heart and understand how best to navigate it.

A Soul mate has spiritually contracted with us to catapult our

egoic consciousness into significant learning, growth, and embodiment of love. Soul mate connections do not need to be romantic
in nature; in fact, some of the most compelling Soul mate relationships are platonic or share some type of creative partnership.
We have spoken to many parents who feel their relationship with
their child is so familiar, it is as if they have known them eternally.
We would call all these relationships Soul mate relationships.

Some Soul mate relationships (whether with a romantic
partner, a child, a neighbor, or even an animal) are so powerful,
they have the ability to jump-start consciousness. No matter how
oblivious or dense our minds may be, the palpable connection
between two Souls can crack through a hardened egoic paradigm.
Have you ever met a stranger who felt like an old friend or experienced an unexplainable chemistry with someone? Sometimes,
first-time meetings are actually Soul reunions. This strong knowing or feeling of remembering is an indication of a potent karmic
Soul-to-Soul relationship.

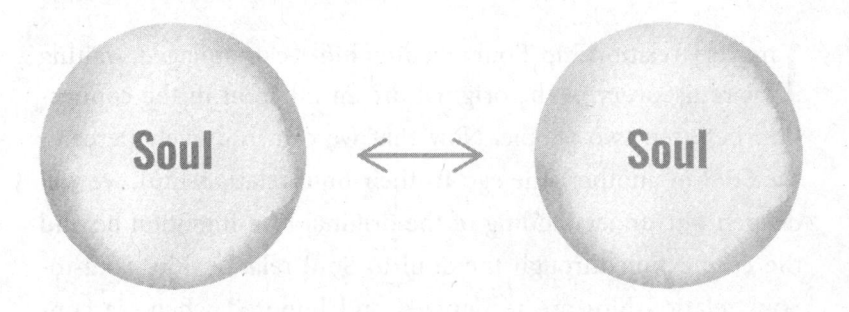

Figure 9. The Soul-to-Soul relationship

These rare and overpowering Soul-to-Soul relationships are
not determined by external factors. What is important to the
ego — social status, physical attraction, or belief systems — has
little effect on a powerful Soul-to-Soul bond. Free of logic or

reason, Soul connection either is or it isn't. Soul knows whom we love, and the why means very little. Soul loves for the quality of a person, their essence, their eternal beauty, or, simply put, their Soul. Most of us, no matter our layers of denial, intuitively sense when we're faced with a powerful Soul-to-Soul relationship. Even if we do not consciously understand what is happening in those sparked moments of familiarity, our gut knows there is something important about the connection. These types of bonds are uncommon; we have found that most people have only a handful of elevated or recognized Soul-to-Soul relationships within a lifetime.

These stronger Soul bonds are characterized by an instinctual deep recognition. We may feel profound connection to a stranger who graces our lives for just a few minutes. We may recognize a strong Soul bond with the mail person or a taxi driver. Other times, Soul bonds can last a lifetime. We often think of these connections as love. We may fall in love, or realize we are already in love, with one of those chosen Souls. We may marry, have children, and live a full life together.

A Soul mate connection is not something we can easily define on the basis of external characteristics; it relies completely on internal awareness. It is in our hands — or, more accurately, our hearts — to decipher what is authentic. Our client Rose describes the night she met her Soul mate and future husband, Asher: "I think about that night a lot because it was the first time I felt attraction to someone that came from someplace deep within me. It definitely did not come from my idea of who I wanted to be with or what I thought was attractive. It had nothing to do with what he looked like or even what he said or did. It was just him. From the moment I saw him, it was just him."

We like to see the unique personalities of Souls as being like different colors. Complementary colors, when combined, make one another seem more vibrant and alive, while noncomplementary colors lose their hue and verve. Similarly, when we are in a relationship with a complementary Soul, we have more confidence, stamina, and passion. When we are with a noncomplementary Soul, our ego may think we are happy, but in reality we feel drained, lackluster, and disconnected from ourselves.

Relationships can either reinvigorate our life force or deplete it. When making this distinction, it is important not to confuse your internal life force with the manic high ego can get from validation. This will require intuitive discernment and Soul dialogue. Asking our Soul first whom we have a strong Soul bond with can serve as our cosmic Match.com and help us find a partner who will bring out the best in us.

One could argue that Beatrice was a strong Soul mate for Dante; they met only briefly, but she became a lifelong muse for him and inspired some of his greatest works, like *The Divine Comedy*. Shams Tabrizi was most definitely a Soul mate for the Sufi poet Rumi, igniting him to compose some of the most profound poetry on mysticism available today. The love relationship between Marie and Pierre Curie, who met at the Sorbonne, produced a scientific collaboration that made huge advances in radiology and resulted in a shared Nobel Prize. Their youngest daughter, Eve, speaks of the mutual reverence between their Souls in her biography *Madame Curie*: "The two souls, like the two brains, were of equal quality." She continues of their union:

> During these happy days was formed one of the finest bonds that ever united man and woman. Two hearts beat together, two bodies were united, and two minds of genius learned to think together. Marie could have married no other than this great physicist, than this wise and noble man; Pierre could have married no woman other than the fair, tender Polish girl, who could be childish or

transcendent within the same few moments; for she was a friend and a wife, a lover and a scientist.

Although sexist attacks were lobbed at Marie from the scientific community of the late 1800s, the Curies disregarded the complaints and dedicated their lives to new creations within science. When Pierre died at the age of forty-six, Marie continued the work and earned a second Nobel Prize.

One of our favorite stories of a predetermined Soul-to-Soul relationship is one we witnessed firsthand through our friends. Lyla, who has a naturally nurturing and generous heart, deeply longed to have a child. She and Mark had been struggling for several years with infertility. Lyla recounts this period as the hardest time of her life. The couple endured years of intense disappointment, wondering month after month whether their baby was ever coming.

During a routine day at work, a coworker announced to Lyla that she was pregnant. After rejoicing with her friend, she got into her car to drive home. Although thrilled for her colleague, Lyla suddenly felt overcome with despair as she grieved the baby missing from her own life. On her long drive home, she became so overwhelmed she had to pull over. As she tells it:

I stopped somewhere, looking at this beautiful countryside, and started to just sob like a crazy person. All of a sudden — I'm not kidding you; it was so weird — there was this crazy rainbow right in front of me! Something about this rainbow gave me hope, like it was a sign. And I remember at that point thinking, "I can't do it this way. I'm not going to be depressed about this. I have to do something." I didn't want to be a victim anymore. So from that moment, I chose to trust that life was unfolding exactly as it should. And when I decided to trust life as it was, I had this feeling, or intuition, that I would have a child.

I just had to trust and be patient. Which was extremely difficulty, seeing that I had no proof my child would ever come. So to help me trust, I started pretending my child was already here. And as ridiculous as that seemed, I remember driving home after that big cry, talking to my child in the back of the car. I did that for many months. At home, I would imagine seeing little red boots running through my yard.

Soon after, the couple found out Mark's job would force them to move to "the middle of nowhere." They would have to live thousands of miles away from their chosen home for the next five years. Lyla was disappointed about the move, but as she was leaving, she told us, in a wistful yet determined voice, "Maybe I will go there and find my baby." We were hopeful her words would come true.

After the move, Lyla and Mark decided they were going to adopt and began looking at different agencies. Finally, the couple settled on one with which they resonated. The agency they chose gave them the task of creating a photo book, designed to give the birth mother a visual glimpse into the lives of the potential new parents.

Lyla and Mark included a recent photo of themselves at an outdoor music festival, listening to one of their favorite bands. The photo stood out to one young mother-to-be. Not only did she feel a warmth from this couple, but they were with her own favorite band.

Lyla and Mark soon received a phone call that there might be a baby for them. Upon the initial meeting with the birth mother, Lyla was overcome by a feeling of Soul recognition. "From the very first moment I saw her [the birth mom] I felt I already knew her," she said. "I remember thinking, 'This is you! I *know you* from somewhere.'"

During this first powerful meeting, they were all shocked to discover that the birth mother and Lyla shared the same birthday: November 11. (Many find the number 11-11 to be spiritually significant as a sign of synchronicity and meaning.) "I try to explain to people just how awesome she is," Lyla says, "and I really can't. I just fell in love with her from the moment I saw her. She just seems so familiar to me, ya know? I don't know. To me it's just magic. Something really magical happened."

Lyla's premonition was right. She had found her baby. Five years later, Mark's job allowed them to move back home, this time as a family. The events in their lives, the seemingly unbearable fertility issues and unsettling move across the country, ended up leading them to a mother who needed their help and a baby who needed a home. If it had not been for the precise step-by-step orchestration of the preceding events, the child might not have found its Soul-aligned parents. When Lyla was imagining and speaking to her child, she was emitting an energetic signal from her Soul that she was ready to be a mom. A child halfway across the nation answered her call, and destiny brought them together. Lyla now often watches the little boots of her child running through her backyard.

Everyone Is Our Teacher

Powerful Soul bonds can overcome us, as these examples show us. What most of us do not realize, though, is that we are surrounded by more subtle Soul-to-Soul relationships all the time. We engage in dozens of Soul relationships every day and in thousands within our lifetime. Underlying every meeting — with our tax accountant, coworkers, librarians, and even the flower vendor we pass on our way to work — is an ethereal Soul-to-Soul connection with the capacity for profound beauty.

When we awaken to the Soulful relationships all around us,

we find not one is devoid of potential purpose. Unlike ego-to-ego relationships, underlying Soul relationships are constantly attempting to teach us invaluable life lessons. On a closer look at the story of Amelia from chapter 6, the seven-year-old who found the courage to face her bully, we see hidden Soul-to-Soul relationships between Amelia and the other girls. What externally seemed pointless and cruel ended up teaching Amelia about her power and sovereignty. The girls' egos may have taunted Amelia, but their Souls were cheering for her to find the love in herself and in them — pushing her, not so gently, into consciousness.

It is true that anyone we meet may be our teacher, whether they are aware of it or not. From inspiring small realizations to stimulating life-altering transformations, the people who show up in our lives are there for a reason. Whether bullies or lovers, the Souls we meet serve as catalysts in our journey to grow our understanding of ourselves. These unexpected teachers may be completely unconscious of their true underlying Soul-to-Soul mission. Their egos may be merely along for the ride, passengers of their Soul's ulterior objective. But there is no doubt these relationships spring from a deep and cosmic love, dedicated to our well-being. This dynamic within a Soul-to-Soul relationship is known as a Soul contract.

A Soul contract is an agreement between two Souls for the development of spiritual growth. All of our relationships and interactions have some degree of a Soul contract, yet some meetings are more charged than others. A common place we find Soul contracts is within families. A child may be teaching their parents the Soul lessons of patience and presence. In contrast, we may have a less significant Soul contract with a barista at our local coffee joint, whose casual conversations teach us Soul lessons of altruism and community. Following is an example of a powerful Soul contract of unconditional love through long-term partnership.

James and Ben had been married more than ten years. Ben had been diagnosed with stage 3 colon cancer. James stood by Ben's side every day of his five-year cancer journey. James never complained about the care and work required of him, other than his obvious heartache from watching Ben living in pain. But despite James's endless ability to caretake, Ben came to believe he had become a burden. Ben tried his best to conceal his pain, emotional and physical, so as not to add to the weight already on James's shoulders. But Ben's sudden withdrawal did not go unnoticed by James, who sensed something was off and booked a session with Elisa.

At the session, Elisa asked Ben to feel the way James's Soul felt about him. Immediately Ben began to cry. "I know, I know, he really loves me," he said. "I just can't believe it sometimes." She then asked Ben to look at how his Soul felt toward James. This only increased Ben's tears of joy: "I love this man so much. I love him more than life itself." They continued to examine the Soul-to-Soul relationship between James and Ben. It was clear that James did not see Ben as a burden in his life but, rather, experienced every moment together as a privilege. It was also obvious that if the situation were reversed, Ben would have gladly done the same for his partner. Ben did not need to feel like a burden because in truth he was a blessing, and the cancer, although incredibly stressful, was helping James to connect to unconditional love. This was the great love lesson behind their Soul contract. Both Ben and James left the session connected to the purity of their love for each other. Ben finally accepted what "unconditionally" really meant.

We start to gather information about the Soul-level nature of a relationship when we ask questions like "What am I meant to learn from this person in this lifetime?," "What is this relationship growing in me?," "How is this relationship helping to turn me into love?," and "How does my Soul feel about their Soul?"

In particular, the response to the last question can be revealing. When we are honest and connected beyond the ego, the Soul's answer can be quite different from how the ego feels. We may believe we have found the perfect relationship, but when we check in with Soul, we see it is not an energetic match. Our ego may interpret someone's actions as mean or bullying, as in the case of seven-year-old Amelia and the girls at her school, yet Soul was able to identify their insecurities and tap into the greater love plan in their relationships. As in the case of Ben, we may have come to believe our mere existence is a burden to someone, while our Soul recognizes we are an essential part of the plan to awaken our partner to love. As we have said, Soul's wisdom is ever changing, depending on the circumstance. Becoming aware of Soul-to-Soul relationships helps us identify whom we want to be with, why people enter our lives, and how they will help us awaken our true nature.

Because of projections, attachment issues, traumas, and misguided beliefs, ego often clouds our true feelings for the Soul standing before us. We may be more aware of our temporal reactive emotions than of our true Soul feelings toward the relationships in our lives. But when we connect on the Soul-to-Soul level, we tap into the original Soul contracts. If we change our interpretation of a conflict from an assault on our identity to a Soul contract for spiritual growth, often the conflict can be quickly rectified. When we bring Soul into the solution, we open to eternal love.

SILENT TOGETHERNESS PRACTICE

Sometimes, our reliance on words and language can actually impede our ability to *see* each other on a Soul level in relationships. Because the ego is often much louder than the Soul, it can be revolutionary to give our egos a time-out and our Souls an opportunity to feel each other without a veil of narrative between us. In this exercise, we practice being together without words so that the language of the heart can be felt.

1. Choose a time when you both have no plans, like a long afternoon or a mellow weekend morning.
2. Try doing some activities together in silence, such as having a meal, washing the dishes, reading, meditating, or going for a walk.
3. When you notice your urge to speak, examine what you want to say and why. Ask yourself: Is this a topic that will bring us closer together or further apart?
4. Bring your awareness to your partner's presence. Notice if you can feel them, even communicate with them, without words. What words are being spoken with your eyes, body language, and energy?
5. You can bring physical touch into this practice as well. Try holding hands, hugging, or exchanging massage. See if you can have a conversation with your bodies. Are you more aware of your partner's energy or essence without words?

SOUL CONTRACTS INQUIRY

Discovering the purpose of the people in our lives is a simple way to wake up to the Soul-to-Soul relationship. Try specifically asking your Soul about the Soul contracts inherent in the relationship. Use the Soul journaling prompts below:

• Soul, what is this relationship changing or growing in me? What am I learning from this person?
• Soul, are there any differences between how my ego and my Soul view this relationship?

- How does my Soul feel about their Soul?
- Soul, how is this relationship turning me into love?
- Is there anything from our history blocking my ability to receive or see their Soul?
- Soul, what do you want me to know about this Soul contract? What is unique about this relationship?

THE FOUR SPIRITUAL RELATIONSHIPS EXERCISE

Now that we understand the Four Spiritual Relationships, let's put them to work. This inquiry allows us to zoom out and view relationship issues as Divine opportunities, helping us to see the Soul lessons and claim the potential for spiritual evolution that they offer.

Choose a current conflict or challenge within a relationship. We are going to examine it from the perspective of each of the four relationships. If this is your first time doing this exercise, start with something small and not too triggering. Complete the following prompts in your journal.

- The conflict I will be investigating today:
- I am frustrated because _____.

The First Relationship: Ego-to-Ego

In this first relationship, we will investigate the egoic interpretation of the conflict, assess communication thus far, and identify any wounds that may be activated. Meditate for a few moments and then answer the following questions in your journal.

- How is this issue perceived by each ego involved?
  - Ego 1:
  - Ego 2:

- Has this issue been communicated? If so, how?
- What are the main wounds being activated? [This is the current understanding from the ego.]
  - Ego 1:
  - Ego 2:

The Second Relationship: Ego-to-Soul

For this portion, we elevate above the ego to access our personal Soul information. We benefit by understanding the Soul's interpretation of what egoic wounds are being activated. Meditate for a few moments and then, through Soul journaling, ask your Soul for its perspective on the conflict:

- Why is this challenge so difficult for me? What is being threatened within me?
- What are the dynamics, feelings, or histories within me that are being activated by this problem?
- Soul, what do you want me to know about this situation?
- What self-care would be helpful in this situation?
- Is there anything my inner child needs to hear or know to feel safe? Is there any action I can take to help my inner child feel comforted?
- Are there any affirmations/mantras that would help me through this?

The Third Relationship: Ego-to-Their-Soul

Now we ask *their* Soul what is going on for them in the situation we are examining. Take a moment to meditate while connecting to their Soul and then Soul journal around the following questions:

- What is going on with them? What are the feelings, thoughts, and belief systems being activated in them?

- Why are they acting this way? Does it come from a past wound or a misunderstanding?
- Why is this challenge so difficult for them? What is being threatened within them?

The Fourth Relationship: Soul-to-Soul

Finally, we reveal the joint Soul lessons overarching the whole Divine orchestration of this conflict.

- What does my Soul tell me about why this is happening?
- What am I learning on a Soul level?
- What are they learning on a Soul level?
- How is the issue giving my ego the potential to grow into a greater version of love?
- How does Love want me to respond to this situation?
- How, specifically, can I be my biggest, most loving self regarding this issue?

MYSTIC MAD LIBS

When we connect to the mystic within, instead of seeing the events of our lives as random, we begin to inquire about the mysterious Soul contracts and lessons behind them. To connect to the Divine orchestration behind circumstance requires a leap of faith. Although tests are hard and often feel "wrong," it doesn't mean your life or even circumstance is actually "wrong." We remind ourselves it is often the most painful situations that grow our Soul the most.

The following writing exercise builds spiritual heft and connects us to the invisible love plan behind the physical circumstances of the material world and the dominant egoic narrative. When faced with a challenging situation, we put on our love goggles and muse on what love could possibly be teaching us. Through this inquiry, we shift from seeing ourselves as a victim of events to being a seeker of a deeper and greater narrative. We begin to become curious about the inherent meaning wanting to reveal itself through the current circumstances of our lives. What might this test ultimately teach you that has the potential to grow you more fully into your Soul?

To begin, think of a challenging situation that has happened in the past or is currently active in your life. (If this is your first time doing the exercise, a past-time example may be a good place to warm up, as current challenges are often more triggering.) Assume there is a greater love plan that exists behind everything. Even if you can't truly believe it at this time, try to suspend judgment while writing to explore that possibility. Then, in your journal, fill in the blanks in the following paragraphs.

The current hard or challenging circumstance that I will be working on today is _____.

Thanks to this challenge, and my newfound discernment, I have become an expert on _____ [the lessons or skill you are becoming a master of].

Because I have lived through this specific test, I am now a teacher of _____ [what you can now share and teach others that you couldn't before]. This situation is specifically and uniquely teaching me _____ [the lessons you have learned from this circumstance].

The Soul contract that I could be learning from and through this may be _____ [the potential spiritual orchestration in this challenge; what your Soul, and other Souls, may be teaching you].

Although I may not be fully healed, I now have permission and understanding to _____ [how you have grown from this circumstance and what newfound wisdom you have gained].

If I knew and embodied _____ [the Soul lesson] completely and totally, I would be freed from the experience of suffering when thinking about this situation.

Because _____ [current challenging circumstance] may be happening, in part, for a loving, mysterious reason, I hypothesize that love may be teaching me _____ [potential Soul lesson].

This challenge is offering the potential for me to become _____ [how you may embody love through this lesson].

While I am in the process of healing, I can take care of myself by _____ [self-care actions].

An affirmation that helps me to feel safe, grounded, and calm today is: _____ [loving affirmation].

SOUL EULOGY

It can be difficult to see the Soul in people we are close to. In our busy everyday lives, we can fall into habituated patterns. We may spend so much of our time just trying to function and get by, the Souls of other people in our lives go unseen.

This next exercise, though potentially intense, has proven to be incredibly effective for our clients. Sometimes the best way to feel someone's Soul is to imagine they are gone. When a person is truly gone, our own attachment issues are not triggered, and we can suddenly see the Soul that we loved with crystal clarity. If we allow ourselves to enter into that awareness now, we can carry it with us every day, while we are still here together with them.

1. Schedule a time with your loved one when you will not be interrupted. Give yourselves plenty of time, because you will need time to process with each other afterward.
2. Go into separate rooms, each with paper and pen or a computer if you prefer typing.
3. Take a moment and imagine your partner has passed away.
4. Now, write their eulogy. Imagine how you would describe who this person was to your community, but also who they were to you personally. What made them uniquely them?
5. After you feel complete in your writing, join together with your loved one and read the eulogies to each other.
6. Take time to verbally process what you each felt as your loved one read your eulogy to you.

CHAPTER 12

Soul Sex

The role of the artist is exactly the same as the role of the lover.
If I love you, I have to make you conscious of the things you don't see.

— JAMES BALDWIN

In intimate partnership, there is no better way to directly experience Soul-to-Soul connection than through Soul sex. During Soul sex we recognize the sanctuary we originally sought in our partners, creating a resurrection of love. We enter an altered state where our bodies become the meeting place for the merging of Souls. Though this may sound like a profound goal achievable only for enlightened lovers, it is not. Soul sex is about showing up in the moment and using the body as a channel for love. Achieving Soul sex starts by answering one simple question: Where does love meet sex?

Sexual Behavior versus Sexual Nature

As we covered earlier, the true personality of our Soul may surprise us. Our Souls may want to paint, sing, or even pursue a degree in law. There is no telling who we will discover when we become aware of our true essence. In Soul sex, this self-discovery continues into the bedroom. We reintroduce ourselves to, or perhaps discover for the first time, our true sexual nature.

It is outwardly apparent that we all have different tastes in food, clothes, hobbies, and lifestyles, but we also have vastly varied sexual natures. Sex is as entirely an individual experience as we are individual Souls. We may want our lover to throw us down onto the bed and ravish us with uncontrollable passion; or we may define sexiness as sharing a candlelit bath. One Soul may swoon when their partner bites their nipple, while another finds it obnoxious and irritating. It may be watching our partner's growing arousal that excites us or perhaps being watched ourselves.

When we allow ourselves to be consumed by authentic desire, we discover our sexual nature is a part of our Soul. What we want in sex, and how we want it, is yet another expression of who we ultimately are. Yet few couples take the time to fully explore their sexual selves. Their unique sexual personalities often go unseen and are never fully realized. Though exploring our erotic individuality is often not associated with spirituality, it is one of the most effective paths to awakening and strengthening our awareness of Soul. Soul lives within our intuitions and impulses, including our sexual ones.

But before we can awaken our true sexual nature, we must shed light on our false sexual behavior. Not all sexual behavior that has made its way into our sex lives comes from the Soul. We may carry sexual trauma that forces us to monitor our desire, addictively seek stimulus, hide our vulnerability, or otherwise emotionally shut down. If we are codependent, we may have become sexual performers, allowing our partner's desires to dictate our actions, rather than coming from our own emotional connection. And often our sexual activities have been influenced by our culture, including media, leading to a mimicking of sexual behavior dissonant from our true sexual nature. When our sexuality comes from these places, we forfeit our chance for Soulful connection.

Not every sexual exchange is a Soulful exchange. Many of us have experienced sex that, although physically satisfying, has left us emotionally empty. Afterward, we feel more distant than close to our partner. If we miss authentic intimacy in sex, often we experience an emotional crash and deep sadness in the moments after orgasm. If we use sex as a distraction from our feelings, they will only resurface as soon as sex is over. Some of us are programmed to habitually race to orgasm. Caught up in libido, sex as performance, or a narrow-vision focus on the end result, we miss the spiritual purpose of the connection completely.

The first step to having Soul sex is identifying what is sexual behavior from our ego versus authentic sexual nature from our Soul. The pivotal question becomes: Would we rather lose ourselves to pleasure or find ourselves within pleasure?

Elisa Speaks

I recently watched a pop singer's performance on a TV awards show. Intricately choreographed and highly sexualized, the performance created a high-energy party atmosphere. The stage erupted with flashing lights, smoke, and colorful laser beams. The audience was in a possessed state of exhilaration.

I was surprised that, even with all the fanfare, I found the show to feel lifeless. Despite the confetti and fireworks, it felt flat and one-dimensional. I did not sense vulnerability or honesty in her movements. Her performance seemed to be based on a persona that had been created, packaged, and delivered to a market audience. I couldn't feel the Soul in her or her music.

I was reminded of how, as an energetically sensitive child, I was intensely aware when I was being watched. One of my first memories was walking down a school hall with children lined up on each side waiting for lunch. I cringed as I had to walk down the middle, feeling all eyes on me. Although I was one of many kids paraded down the middle, I still dreaded this energetic running of the gauntlet. I much preferred to be part of the crowd, in the role of watcher instead of watched.

Later, when I turned twenty-five, I went with some girlfriends to a bachelorette party. We were signed up to take a pole dancing class; it was going to be hilarious! We arrived in the dim candlelit studio, and a brunette woman came out and began to move slowly onto the pole. The hyper and superficial vibe of the bachelorette party quickly melted away; something entranced us all in her graceful, powerful movements. It did not feel like she was performing; rather, her vulnerability and authenticity created a sacred space. She was moving slowly, sensually, definitely sexually, but she was not gearing her movements toward what the audience would think was sexy. She was led by her own sexual nature. These movements belonged to her, originating from her alone and performed for herself. And if anyone wanted to marvel, they could, but it was clear she would change herself for no one.

I was surprised to notice tears running down my cheeks. I had never seen anything sexual that was also so raw, authentic, honest, and expressive as this. I understood then that I had not yet found my own sexual presence. I was witnessing something true, and I had no idea how to be watched in that level of truth. I realized I did not want to hide anymore.

I immediately signed up for the intro class. The first day was cringeworthy. I laughed nervously, awkwardly contorting my body like a puppet, shame boiling up in my chest. Even with my background in modern dance, dancing in a way that was summoning sexual energy felt embarrassing. The cultural sexual shadow had been projected on me so long that I had become disconnected from my natural sensuality. I saw that I had to break performative habits — "trying to be sexy" — in order to discover my true sexual nature and expression.

Over time, I became comfortable with the power of my Soul speaking sensually through my body. I felt my authentic self, with no separation between my ego and Soul moving through me. I was finally me, no longer performing, ready to be witnessed. Now I didn't mind being watched. I wanted to be seen.

We can identify ego sex versus Soul sex in the same way we differentiate the dances Elisa described above. The key question is: Is this sexual exchange performative in nature, or is this a true meeting place where the Soul selves are exposed and expressed? Soul sex requires that we remain connected to our inner authenticity. In sex it can be easy for our identity to be swept away by the feverish desires of another. If we are unaware of projective identification, we may match or become the object of our partner's egoic desire. But with a simple emotional check-in with ourselves, we can realign with our Soul and meet our partner on a deeper level. Instead of giving our partner what their ego wants, we give them what their Soul needs.

During Soul sex, we become aware of our fear of being visible. When we are truly seen, it can feel scary and uplifting at the same time. It is partially up to us to allow ourselves to be seen, but it is equally important for our partner to seek our true self. The beholder and the beheld enter a spiritual state together.

Unconditional Foreplay

Most people believe sex begins in the bedroom, but sex begins with the energetic relationship we cultivate in our daily lives. Soul sex doesn't start when he leans forward to kiss her but when he takes out the trash. Soul sex is not initiated when she takes off her clothes but when she lights up as he walks through the door. Talking, sitting together in silence, and going for a walk can all be forms of energetic preparation for Soul sex. Any activity can set the energetic mood, so to speak, if we are present, intimate, and in a state of unconditional love together. This may sound simple enough, yet couples rarely are emotionally available to bask in a state of absolute acceptance and unconditionality. If we cannot reach this state in our daily lives, we certainly cannot attain it in the bedroom. But we can build up to this state of being through what we like to call unconditional foreplay.

Unconditional foreplay consists of daily acts, no matter how small, done with pure love. These acts show our partners — and convince their nervous system — that they are safe and cared for. These small, yet powerful, loving acts slowly permit our partner to enter a state of receiving true love. Our acts of love are defined, not by *what* we do, but by *how* we do them.

What may look externally like an unconditional act may in truth be conditional. If we are motivated by codependency, needing approval or seeking an emotional reward from our partner, our action remains conditional, and so does our sex. The difference has everything to do with intention, with the energy underlying the act. For instance, if we buy flowers for our partner because we are motivated by the desire for approval, it is a conditional (or inherently fear-based) act. We are giving them a gift in exchange for affection; it is an attempt to purchase love. We may even get upset with our partner if they do not like the flowers or they do not give us the egoic validation we want. Conditional love has rules and expectations.

But this same act, while looking identical on the outside, can also be motivated by Soul's unadulterated love. In unconditional acts, we celebrate our love. We do not ask our partners to be personal stewards of approval; rather, we give love freely. We do not love our partners merely because they make us feel good but because we see and champion the unique beauty of their Souls. In unconditional relationship we do not addictively chase a particular feeling but rejoice in another's simple existence. We do not attempt to control our partner's feelings so that we feel better ourselves; we simply love, endlessly.

If we want to elevate sex into authentic Soul union, we must start by living authentically, as Soul, in daily relationship. Our sexual issues of disconnection do not originate or heal in the bedroom but in the daily minutiae of our lives. If we want Holy Love to visit us in bed, we must nurture it outside of the bedroom. Couples often live in an ego-to-ego relationship all day long and then feel disappointed when they don't have meaningful, mind-blowing sex at night. This leads couples to assume they have physical intimacy issues when in truth their discord is a result of avoiding emotional intimacy in their everyday interactions. The old Zen saying "How you do one thing is how you do everything" teaches us to be mindful of how we show up in all areas of our lives. If, at 5 p.m., we ask our partner in a rushed and urgent manner about the details of the bank account, at 10 p.m. the bedroom vibe will most likely be rushed and urgent. To enter an unconditional state of union, we must use spiritual information paired with real-world action.

Many of us have blocks to receiving Holy Love, especially if we were neglected, abandoned, or rejected in relationships before. Daily acts of unconditional love allow even the deepest wounds of intimacy to heal. Such acts calm our base emotional needs — such as the need for safety — while bringing down to earth the spiritual potential of Holy Love. The result is a mutual spiritual trust that deepens over time. In the words of the famed theologian Beatrice Bruteau, "Love seeks the ultimately *real*." This *real* truth is found, Bruteau writes, by "an outflowing action of loving another person." When we create the environment of love within our relationships, we open space for the Soul to come forth.

We do not necessarily need unconditional foreplay to have Soul sex. At times Soul may possess us with love. Soul may find a window in which our wounds are not triggered, anxiety is low, and hearts are open. But these moments are dependent on circumstance. If we wish to have a conscious and regular practice of Soul sex, we must begin by implementing loving actions in our relationship. When we see through the eyes of Soul in intimate relationship, every action (or lack of action) carries weight. Every act in relationships is either spiritual foreplay (increasing the ability to receive unconditionality) or distancing (increasing the belief in conditionality). From this vantage point, any time spent together becomes an opportunity for unconditional foreplay.

Touching the Divine

Once we spiritually warm up into a state of unconditional love, we are ready to touch the Soul in another. Now, as we approach sex itself, we prepare our senses to sexually engage body and Soul. We learn to speak without our words, intuitively, through our bodies.

Our desire to touch Divinity is not new. Humans have been embarking on pilgrimage with this same desire since the dawn of religion. Pilgrims flock to touch the Rock of Calvary where Jesus Christ was allegedly crucified. Buddhists pilgrimage to sites associated with great teachers, where they believe the veil between this reality and the ultimate reality of Nirvana has worn thin. Pilgrims seeking healing submerse themselves in the sacred waters of the Lourdes spring in France. As long as humanity has believed in the sacred, we have sought to feel, touch, and experience the Divine.

We all have this quiet yet powerful calling in our hearts to seek Divine connection. The spiritual author and teacher Caroline

Myss describes this calling as a Divine seduction in her book *Entering the Castle*:

> You have a biological and spiritual need to experience the awe of the sacred. That is why we put sacred objects on our desk and nightstands, perform rituals, and travel to ancient temples, ashrams, and churches where saints are buried. We want to touch the sacred and feel its energy, to connect to it personally and connect to it through our purpose. The divine calls to us through these places, actions, and objects, constantly seducing us.

This calling toward Divinity seems to be wired into our DNA. To touch the Soul of our partner, we must align our inherent pilgrim's call with our sexual urge.

Before we even touch our partners, we must examine the nature of the call within us. We have to determine our true motives pulling us to have sex. Are we acting on a *physical call* to orgasm, a *wounded call* to seek approval, a *codependent call* to neurotically help our partner feel better? Or is it the *pilgrim's call* to feel, touch, and experience a greater love? We define *pilgrim*, in this sense, as "an individual who journeys to a spiritual place for mystical or holy reasons." As pilgrims of Soul sex, we journey behind the veil to tangibly feel, touch, and make love with Divinity.

Most people do not understand the potential of sex. We sense it is destined to be more than mere physical penetration but have yet to define what this "more" is. For many, sex is an arena where comparing and competition still exist. If ego is convincing, controlling, counting, or comparing sexual encounters, a huge spiritual opportunity is missed. Through the lens of ego, sex is purely performative and ultimately only a place to experience physical release and stimulation, like a glorified sneeze.

The "more" that elevates physical sex to spiritual sex is Soulful connection. This form of sex connects us to the heart of each other and the Divine. Sex becomes an alchemical vessel: a place of meeting and solace where we surrender to love and are transformed. If we allow it, life (and sex) on earth leaves the rat race behind and enters into a field of potential grace. The level of Soul connection in bed determines the degree of Divinity penetrating our sex. We have a natural longing for authentic presence to wake us up during sex. If we disconnect, we become susceptible to cold and Soulless physical penetration. After a shallow sexual encounter, we leave unchanged, as self-focused as before it began, continuing to experience life on autopilot. If we have a Soul exchange during sex, time stops and we are initiated. We experience the world as more alive, benevolent, and inherently interconnected. It is completely our choice if we seek unconscious or conscious sex.

Similarly, the pilgrim could also travel to a holy site unconsciously and arrive to find no Divine encounter at all. Stuck in material literalism, they may touch the Rock of Calvary and feel the same as if they touched a rock in their own backyard. It is the intention and the inner listening that elicit a mystical experience through and within sacred places. No matter how far away we are from a mystic site, when we listen to the call, we've already begun to prepare ourselves to experience the mystical once we arrive. By adhering to the call, we create a portal to Divinity within these sites.

As in other aspects of relationship, intention is paramount in our sexual encounters. Our intention and motive before we engage in sex determine the quality of our sex. Like pilgrims, we do not need to know all the answers before we depart on our journey. We do not need to be sexual mind readers, tantra masters, or seers who can view the aura of the person in front of us. We need only to follow the calling toward finding Divinity in another. We are no longer asking what love would say but "How does love touch?," "How would love move?," and, ultimately, "What does it feel like to become love?" Asking these questions inherently alters the intention of the lovemaking. We leave behind comparison to experience a miracle. When we enter this state of surrender to the Divine seduction, we open a magic door within our partners. This door is an opening to the Soul.

Soul Sensations

The energy of Soul within the body may arise in a multitude of sensations: it can be a tingling in our hearts, a rush of ecstasy down our spine, heat in our fingertips, or pleasure flowering in our chests. To increase our awareness of these energetics, we can begin identifying where we already experience the somatic, or physical, sensations of love in our lives: when we see someone we love from afar and our hearts swell with happiness, for example, or when we blow a kiss to our children, or when we send an air hug over a Skype call to relatives. Love is an energy emitting from our Souls. We can give and receive this love energy through awareness and intention.

The first step to feeling energy is quieting the mind and opening our awareness. Once Adam attended a ten-day meditation retreat. The strictly enforced rules of the ashram were no external distractions (including books, TV, and music), no eye contact with other participants, and no talking for the entire duration of the stay. Limiting external stimuli was intended to awaken an internal awareness in the participants. The style of meditation itself was entirely focused on becoming present with the current experience in the body. The first day began with bringing awareness to the nearly indetectable sensation of breath passing over the upper lip from the nose. On the morning of this first day, Adam felt only a slight cool tingling. By the end of the week, however, the inhale and exhale felt like waves bringing an entire ocean of sensations with every breath.

Similarly, feeling energetic sensations within sex is a skill that grows with awareness. When we attune and listen, we will notice that Soul is speaking through a complicated and nuanced language of sensations. Energetics is the language the Soul emits at all times. The key to deciphering this language is using intuition and the Four Spiritual Relationships. We've included in-depth exercises at the end of this chapter to help you increase awareness of energetics in sex and develop a shorthand for receiving intuitive information and guidance.

Intuition is required in Soul sex because every body is different and needs its own unique somatic medicine. During sex, we may be called to do the most particular and even peculiar somatic work. Our Soul may instruct us to pause and gently pound on our partner's chest, or shake and loosen up trauma in their knees, or massage between their shoulder blades to free a deeply held pattern of stress. Every cell of our body holds stories from our past that can be reactivated under certain conditions. It is a blessing when we can access those old feelings to release them from the body. It is crucial to enter into Soul sex with absolutely no judgment and to trust in each other's intuitive moments.

Our ego, especially in sex, may want to ignore the subtle cues of intuitive and somatic guidance to get its desired approval. But if we do this, we will miss the spiritual potential of sex altogether. When we *do* utilize the Four Spiritual Relationships and listen to Soul's wisdom, we slowly melt the layers of resistance to true intimacy. In the introduction of this book, we claimed that creating this true intimacy between two people is more profound than most realize. Now, we will discover why.

YOUR PILGRIM'S CALL

The archetype of the pilgrim is the individual who journeys to a spiritual place for mystical or holy reasons. The purpose of the exercise below is to become clear about your pilgrim's call — your spiritual intentions — in relation to sexual energy. What are you truly seeking in sexual intimacy and exchange, and what is the final spiritual destination you hope to reach? As we elevate our sex into the realm of energetic healing, intention becomes our greatest tool — and our greatest challenge. Unless we are honest with ourselves and our partners about our motive for seeking sex in the first place, we may miss the spiritual opportunity altogether.

The following Soul journaling prompts help us to assess any unconscious objectives so that we may clear and release them. The last questions focus on becoming aligned with the Soul's desire for true union.

- Soul, what does my ego want from sex?
- Soul, is there any wound I am looking to distract myself from or to fuel? If yes, what is the wound? What does this wound need to know, hear, or feel?
- Soul, what does my partner's ego want from sex?
- Soul, am I codependently reacting to what my partner wants in sex?
- Soul, what does my Soul want in sex?
- Soul, what does my partner's Soul want from sex?
- Soul, do I feel permission to communicate how I feel and what I desire to my partner?
- Soul, what would you like to say about my sexual nature to my partner?
- Soul, what intention do you want to set before having sex?
- Soul, when sexual energy is activated and I am engaging in it, am I being myself? Soul, do I allow myself to feel my true feelings in the present moment? If not, why not?
- Soul, do I feel the need to perform, or am I allowing my vulnerability in the room?
- Soul, do I currently have any sexual habits or behaviors that are not emerging from or aligned with my Soul?

- Soul, do I have any shame or cultural or religious programming around sex? Can I envision a God that is supportive and encouraging of my natural sexual energy? Can I perceive my sexual nature as coming from and serving God / the Creator / the Divine?
- If there is shame to clear, how do you want me to heal or work on this?
- Soul, because we store trauma in our physical bodies, is there any action, affirmation, or ritual that would help me to reclaim sovereignty and bring healing to my own sexual organs?
- Soul, where does my sexual nature come from? What is the Soul's motive behind sex?
- Soul, is there anything else you want me to learn about myself sexually?

RED LIGHT, GREEN LIGHT

This is an exercise to remove false sexual programming and help you to practice authentic alignment between your physical body and your Soul. You may remember a game from your childhood called Red Light, Green Light. Everyone starts in a line at one end of the playing field, with the exception of a designated traffic patrol, who stands at the opposite end. When the traffic patrol yells, "Green light!" everyone runs toward them; but if they yell, "Red light," everyone has to stop immediately. If you accidentally move or trip over yourself from your own momentum, you have to return to the starting line. The goal is to be the first one to reach the traffic patrol at the finish line. To play well, you have to listen intently and be aware of your own physical speed.

In our version, Soul will be the traffic patrol giving directives. Before sex even begins, ask your Soul to show you the image of a classic traffic signal with a red light on top, yellow in the middle, and green on the bottom. (There is no yellow light in the children's game, but we have added it in for the sake of the exercise.) We are going to use the power of imagination during sex to have a conversation with Soul via the metaphor of the traffic lights.

When you're ready to talk with your Soul, just as in Soul dialoguing, take a moment to intuitively check in with your higher self. Set the intention of receiving intuitive symbols in answer to your questions. Now, ask Soul to let you know — via the red, yellow, or green light — how things are going in bed. If you find it challenging to receive the answer as an image in the mind, know that it can also be received as words, emotions, or somatic symptoms. We all have different intuitive strengths and can receive information in a variety of ways.

This practice uses symbolic shorthand to quickly convey Soul information. As we become familiar with the practice, it serves as somatic biofeedback to bridge our physical experience with the feelings of Soul. During sex, every now and then, take a moment to check in with your Soul. Ask to see the symbol of either a red, a yellow, or a green light. Here are the meanings behind each:

- **Red light:** Stop. Take a moment to identify what is out of alignment. Before you enter into sex again, ask Soul, "Why did you show me a red light?" If the answer is difficult to receive, ask Soul, "How am I feeling right now? How is my partner feeling?" Do not initiate sex again until you get the go-ahead from your Soul.
- **Yellow light:** Proceed with caution and compassion; you are now in healing territory. A yellow light means you and your partner have entered a new vulnerable depth with each other that you may not be accustomed to. It is important to have a positive experience at this point,

even if this stage is accompanied by difficult emotional releases. Hold space for each other; do not rush through it. Actively listen to Soul for guidance.

- **Green light:** Enjoy yourself. The green light is a sign you are on the right track. Allow Soul to continue to guide and move you. We may receive a green light from our Soul when an unexpected experience arises in sex, like vulnerability, and Soul wants us to continue. In short, green light stands for trust in oneself and a surrender into the moment and into love. But remember, we may get a green light, and within moments the color may change. Green light is not an excuse to disconnect from Soul's guidance. Continue to check in, every now and again, as you proceed.

MYSTICAL CHAIRS

Mystical Chairs is an exercise that we often use at retreats. We set up a couple facing each other in two chairs and provide a topic for them to talk about. This is usually a recent conflict in their relationship. We ask the couple to pay close attention to their intuitive and somatic reactions to each statement their partner makes. If one partner says something that the other feels is untrustworthy or untrue, they move their chair a foot away. If their partner says something that activates trust and intimacy in their body, they move their chair a foot closer.

What is fascinating about this game is that most couples find they have an average amount of space between them that they cannot in full honesty cross, usually anywhere between one foot and twenty feet. The distance between their chairs is a symbolic representation of the emotional distance between them. In the Red Light, Green Light game, we could call this the yellow zone:

a place that is in need of healing before they can achieve spiritual intimacy. In Soul-led sex, we are closing this emotional gap.

With your partner, experiment with this exercise to visually assess the amount of space that needs healing in order for you to experience deeper intimacy.

1. Sit in two chairs facing each other, about four feet apart.
2. Choose a topic that has recently caused a conflict in your relationship.
3. Take turns stating how you felt during the disagreement and what you felt was left unsaid or unheard.
4. After your partner says a statement, notice your emotional state. Do you feel more or less intimate with your partner? Do you feel closer to or further from them? If you feel less intimate, move your chair back a foot. If you feel more intimate, move your chair a foot closer.
5. Notice why you moved your chair away. Was it what they said or how they said it? See if you can pinpoint the specific reason you moved your chair back. Share this information with your partner.
6. Notice why you moved your chair closer. Was it because what they said was true, seemed vulnerable, or felt authentic? Share this information with your partner.
7. See if you can now say statements to each other that bring your chairs closer.
8. After the exercise, discuss your experience with your partner. See if you can identify whether it was the conflict itself that made you feel distant from each other or something else. If it is difficult to locate the right words for these answers (or if you ended up with your chairs across the room from each other), do some Soul journaling to process the experience further and then share the results.

SEX WITHOUT TOUCH

The following three-part exercise is designed to awaken your senses to the subtleties of energy. It is also a great way to warm up the senses for sex itself and can be used during energetic foreplay. We are often surprised at how the seemingly elusive, culturally minimized reality of experiencing energetics can be easily and quickly accessed by almost anyone with conscious intent and focused awareness. Our Souls are always speaking to each other, but not always in words. Energetics is the language the Soul emits at all times; all we have to do is listen. This exercise will help you and your partner learn how to listen and respond through feeling. We hope it opens up an entirely new way of being with your partner sexually and also in daily life.

Part 1: The Pilgrim

Both partners should do the following steps simultaneously.

1. Find a comfortable place to sit across from each other at arm's length distance.
2. On your own, tap your fingers together (like you are clapping with your fingertips) for about fifteen to thirty seconds.
3. Shake your hands as if you are shaking water off them.
4. Rub your own hands together and set the intention to shoot love out of the center of your palms.
5. Imagine the feeling of love coming out of the center of your palms. If it helps, ask your Soul for a color that symbolizes your love and imagine this color coming out your hands.
6. Hold your hands up a few inches away from your partner's palms.

7. Take turns practicing pushing your love toward the other while the other receives your love. Notice what you feel. See if you can feel a difference in the sensation when you change the intention of who is pushing and who is receiving.

Part 2: The Missionary

1. Lie next to each other without physically touching.
2. To begin, you will give the energy and your partner will receive. Have your partner close their eyes while you imagine your love coming out of your palms. Run your hands over their body without touching them, initially keeping your hands about a foot away. Have your partner give verbal feedback on what and where they feel sensations while they keep their eyes closed. Practice moving your hands further and closer, still without actually touching. Find the distance where your partner begins to feel you. When you are ready, switch roles and repeat.
3. Now, place your hands over each other's hearts. Both partners can now close their eyes. Have one partner think about what they love most about the other. Try to remember the feeling from your happiest memories together, but do not talk — just focus on the feeling. Have the other partner give verbal feedback on what they experience, trying to be specific about the sensations. Switch when you are ready.

Part 3: The Prophet

1. This next exercise can be done lying next to each other or standing up face-to-face. Take a moment to shake off any tension. Shake out the hands as if you are drying them off.

Next shake the arms, legs, feet, and torso. We are waking up the energy system and bringing movement into any parts of the body where energy may be stagnant.

2. Set the intention to allow Soul to guide you.
3. Set the intention to allow your partner's Soul to guide you.
4. Place your hands palm to palm a few inches apart, without touching.
5. See if you can allow your energy to guide your hands. Where on your partner are your hands drawn? How do you want to move them? Where do you want to caress your partner? Without touching their body, let your hands glide over your partner, led by your energy.
6. If you are the partner in the receptive role, notice when you feel a push or a pull from your partner's energy as it flows through their hands. Allow your body to move correspondingly.
7. See if you can get your energetic movements to sync up — in other words, see if you can both follow where the energy wants to lead. Without overthinking it, allow whatever sensations, intuitive information, or loving impulses arise to move you and your partner.

SOUL SEX GUIDELINES

We have covered many of the techniques for Soul sex in this chapter. Below is a quick reference guide for achieving Soul union in sex. These are all tools to help move you toward Soul intimacy, but in and of themselves, they will not create Soul union. Remember, the most important tool for Soul union is love. An element of grace will come into a sexual union that is aligned with higher love. The most we can do is focus our minds and open our hearts. The tips and tricks listed here will help us get out of our own way and learn to love as our Soul naturally and already knows how to.

1. **Pray.** Pick whichever name feels best to you and repeat this prayer: "Universe, God, Unconditional Love, Beloved, I am ready to experience Soul union with my loved one. I am ready to know them; I am ready to be known. Let our Souls rejoice within each other; let us know true love together through sex. Let us meet with love, in love, as love. Thank you."

2. **Set your intention.** Place a hand on your heart and repeat this phrase with authentic intention and willingness: "I want to experience Soul union with [partner's name]. I am ready to experience Soul union with [name]. I will know [name's] Soul. I will know [name] as love."

3. **Follow the energy.** Authentic movement is moving the body *the way it wants to move* instead of forcing it to move from an idea, from your headspace. Some refer to this as feeling as though you are "being danced" instead of dancing. See if you can move and have sex from where you enjoy the experience of being in the flow. Notice when you are in the energy of what your body wants to be doing and when you are pushing, forcing, or resisting where your body wants to go. Get in sync with what your Soul wants over what your ego wants by following the pulse of your own energy and your partner's.

4. **Drop the role for Soul.** If we enact a role during sex, we will feel lack during or after the act. Especially after orgasm, it is often very clear what role the sexual experience relied upon. If you are playing a part (which is especially tempting if you are an empath), you will feel defeated, disconnected, withdrawn, or sad after sex. If, on the other hand, you connect to your Soul and the Soul of

your partner during sex, then after it's over, you will feel
closer to your partner and connected to your authentic
self. Whenever you feel disconnected, place a hand on
your heart and ask Soul, "Am I being myself?"

5. **Notice your feelings.** It can be easy to get caught up in
    a sexual act, so it is essential to continually check in and
    notice how you are actually feeling. If you are experienc-
    ing a nagging feeling that something is not right, it prob-
    ably isn't. If you feel uncomfortable, ask yourself what is
    going on and if you can do anything about it. Sex is a
    common place to retraumatize yourself if you cut your-
    self off from what your Soul is telling you.

6. **Know that it's OK to stop and reconnect.** Avoid the
    pressure to race to orgasm. It is common to get trapped
    into pleasing if you are coming from a role rather than
    your authentic self. It's also common to get overly focused
    on the physical aspects of sex. Instead, stay with Soul. To
    avoid hyperfocusing on the sexual organs, expand your
    awareness and notice how your legs and feet are feeling
    or your heart center. Somatic awareness brings you into
    the moment and out of your heady ideas or sexual pro-
    gramming. Don't let the heat of the moment turn down
    the heat from the Soul.

CHAPTER 13

Soul Communion

There are only two ways to live your life. One is as though nothing is a miracle. The other is as though everything is a miracle.

— ALBERT EINSTEIN

Everything in this book has been designed to prepare you and your partner for the final destination of Soul communion. Soul communion is not something that can be forced. Similarly to writing a hit song or painting a masterpiece, we can't always predict when inspiration or artistic genius may strike, but we can create the conditions and space for the creative spark to move us. By applying what we know about the Four Spiritual Relationships, we prepare our minds, bodies, and Souls for an ecstatic and holy experience through intimacy. Then, grace and Divine timing allow spiritual experiences to occur.

We started our journey by recognizing the longing in our hearts to know a Holy Love. This longing to experience genuine intimacy and union has inherent within it the deeper impulse to reestablish connection to the Divine. Which may bring up the questions: Why were we separated from Holy Love in the first place? Why did we have to work so hard to find unconditional love through the conditional, reactive, and deceptive ego? Why have we been submitting to the challenging and often heartbreaking lessons that come with relationships?

God is love, eternal and unconditional. What separates this Divine and Holy Love from an ordinary love is the unconditional. *Unconditional* means "absolute, unqualified, and never-ending." Such an infinite love is difficult for us in our egoic identity to truly understand. Yet anytime we participate in unconditional love, we participate in God. We are fortunate if we embody this state of pure love even for a moment. And though God may be beyond our comprehension, there is a part of us that recognizes love. This is the simple and profound truth: intimacy is a sacred path to God.

It is easy to turn relationship work into a self-improvement project. We may believe we need to become "better people" to give and receive love unconditionally. But the truth is, we do not need to *do* anything or prove ourselves to be worthy of Holy Love. There are no conditions on who is worthy of the unconditional — good or bad, conscious or unconscious, wise or unwise. Unconditional love is, by definition, just that — without conditions.

In a self-created paradox, if we believe we need to "improve" ourselves before we can know love, we inadvertently block ourselves from it. We seek a love we had access to all along. In Soul-led relationships, we may be encouraged to grow and change, but not because we do not deserve unconditional love already, as we are. Spiritual intimacy does not change our nature; it teaches us to accept it. We become aware of the unconditional love that already radiates from our Soul. Holy Love is the most natural expression of our existence. When two Souls recognize and take guidance from this love, they enter into a state of communion.

So at the end of our journey, we find ourselves at the beginning. Through all of our spiritual work, we come to realize that we never had to change ourselves to enter the field of Holy Love in the first place. The purpose of the Four Spiritual Relationships is not to become worthy of love but to become conscious of love. We teach each other, through Soul-guided words and actions, what unconditional love really is. And in this way, we teach each other what God really is.

Being in Love Is Being in God

We are born with a calling in our hearts to find, give, and receive unconditional God with another person. Our impulse to love is our impulse to God. Authentic intimacy is God seeking the conscious, ecstatic experience of itself. When we touch, witness, and make love to the Soul of another, we align with and embody Divinity. In the words of the mystic poet Rumi, "The way you make love is the way God will be with you."

God is like a river we cannot grasp hold of. God's elusive substance will pass right through our fingertips. But we *can* feel the flow of God's presence by holding each other. We swim in Divine waters by entering into a state of unconditional love and Soul communion together.

Soul communion is achieved when we experience, even temporarily, a love so great that we touch the holy. The closer we get to each other in love, the closer we get to God. Instead of chasing God "out there," we seek a love "in here." We stop searching for a distant and separate God and begin to honor the loving impulses within us as God. Seeking God becomes the answer to the question, Where is the love right here, right now?

We have achieved a moment of holiness between two Souls when the touch of our partner's hand releases an exhalation of breath, the expulsion of our worries, and a rush of relief. We know Holy Love when a moment of intimacy makes us gasp and whisper to the heavens, "Thank you." We experience Holy Love when in an embrace we feel the membrane between us and the Divine begin to wear thin. We feel Holy Love when we share our hardships with another, weep in each other's arms until we release our pain, and discover a newfound peace. We sense Holy Love when we feel so utterly and completely seen and met by our lover that we are satiated to the core of our being. We are in Holy Love when we say, "I love you" and know it as an eternal truth. We have achieved perfect Holy Love when we finally know, from experience and without hesitation, that yes, God is love, but also love is God.

Acknowledgments

We would like to thank Georgia Hughes, our editor at New World Library. We are so glad *Holy Love* spoke to you and appreciate your work bringing it into the world. Additional thanks to Diana Rico and Kristen Cashman for your editing detail and improvements on the manuscript.

Thank you to Rachel Rothberg, the incredible artist and creator of the beautiful owl cover image.

We would also like to thank our agent, Wendy Sherman, for your support and encouragement.

To our "it takes a village" pod, Kasia, Michael, Eli, Laurel, Kyle, and Freya: thank you so much for being truly amazing friends and Soul family.

Thank you, Mom, for your editing and for consistently showing up.

And thank you to our clients whose stories have graced our hearts and these pages. We deeply appreciate your part in helping bring *Holy Love* to all those ready to receive it.

Notes

Chapter 2: Holy Lovers Are Mystics

p. 16   *At times, high EQ and SQ*: Danah Zohar and Ian Marshall, *SQ: Connecting with Our Spiritual Intelligence* (New York: Bloomsbury, 2000), 10.

Chapter 5: The Ego-to-Soul Relationship

p. 57   *"Life is not a problem"*: Joseph Campbell, *The Hero's Journey* (Novato, CA: New World Library, 2014), xvii.

p. 60   *"Call the world, if you please"*: John Keats, *The Letters of John Keats, 1814–1821*, ed. Hyder Edward Rollins (Cambridge, MA: Harvard University Press, 1958), 100–102.

Chapter 7: Healing the Inner Child

p. 96   *"Only the soul knows"*: Rumi, *The Soul of Rumi: A New Collection of Ecstatic Poems*, trans. Coleman Barks (San Francisco: HarperOne, 2002), 204.

p. 98   *"I believe that appreciation"*: Fred Rogers (commencement speech, Marquette University, Milwaukee, May 2001), https://www.marquette.edu/university-honors/honorary-degrees/rogers-speech.php.

Chapter 8: Tough Love

p. 109 *Carl Jung likened this process*: Carl G. Jung, *Memories, Dreams, Reflections* (New York: Pantheon Books, 1961), 357.

Chapter 9: Meet Their Soul

p. 130 *"biography becomes biology"*: Caroline Myss, *Anatomy of the Spirit: The Seven Stages of Power and Healing* (New York: Harmony Books, 1996), 42.

Chapter 10: Seeing the Soul

p. 136 *"Awakening happens when you stop"*: Adyashanti, quoted in Luc Saunders and Sy Safransky, "Who Hears This Sound? Adyashanti on Waking Up from the Dream of 'Me,'" *The Sun*, December 2007, https://www.thesunmagazine.org/issues/384/who-hears-this-sound.

p. 136 *"Man has no body"*: William Blake, *The Poetical Works of William Blake*, ed. John Sampson (London, New York: Oxford University Press, 1908), 240.

p. 140 *"Do you know that even when"*: Jiddu Krishnamurti, *Freedom from the Known* (London: Ebury Publishing, 2010), 25.

p. 142 *In 1955 a group of monks*: Peter McKenzie-Brown, "The Golden Buddha and the Man Himself," Language Matters, May 7, 2007, https://languageinstinct.blogspot.com/2007/05/golden-budda-and -man-himself.html.

Chapter 11: The Soul-to-Soul Relationship

p. 160 *"The two souls, like the two brains"*: Eve Curie, *Madame Curie: A Biography* (Boston: Da Capo Press, 2001), 141.

p. 160 *"During these happy days"*: Curie, *Madame Curie*, 141.

Chapter 12: Soul Sex

p. 181 *"Love seeks the ultimately real"*: Beatrice Bruteau, "Persons in Love," *The Roll*, March 1996, 9–10.

p. 183 *"You have a biological and spiritual need"*: Caroline Myss, *Entering the*

Castle: Finding the Inner Path to God and Your Soul's Purpose (New York: Free Press, 2007), 149.

Chapter 13: Soul Communion

p. 199   *"The way you make love"*: Rumi, *The Book of Love: Poems of Ecstasy and Longing*, trans. Coleman Barks, repr. (New York: HarperOne, 2005), 69.

About the Authors

Elisa Romeo is a licensed marriage and family therapist, intuitive, and bestselling author of *Meet Your Soul: A Powerful Guide to Connect with Your Most Sacred Self*. After meeting her Soul during an out-of-body experience, she uncovered an ability to see and communicate with the Soul energy of others, including Souls who have crossed over. She teaches others how to connect to the still-small voice of intuition in order to access their ultimate and eternal love self. Her worldwide private practice, which grew by word of mouth, consists of thousands of clients, whom she works with by merging her background in depth psychology with an ability to directly communicate with the Soul.

While living in India, **Adam Foley** found himself in the wrong place at the wrong time: trapped in the center of a large-scale terrorist bombing. As he was the lone American at the scene, news stories highlighted his nationality, which brought unwanted attention from the terrorists and ultimately compromised his personal safety. He wrestled with the injustice of fate after surviving this experience while others did not. Seeking existential answers and anonymity, he traveled around India, trained with

world-renowned gurus, and became a certified somatic prac-
titioner and yoga instructor. Yet it wasn't until Adam met Elisa
that he experienced himself as a Soul and understood the eternal nature of love. As a healer, he uses spiritual coaching, somatic
healing, and his own intuitive abilities to connect people to their
Souls.

Together, Elisa and Adam help individuals awaken and
deepen their Soulful nature within relationship. As married parents of two, they use practical stories from the trenches of everyday life to teach sacred partnership, as well as their personal
spiritual experiences and examples from their work with thousands of couples. They show that the spiritual journey can be as
simple — and profound — as getting closer to the people we love.
With relationship as a spiritual path, we discover that instead of
giving or receiving love, we become love itself.

Adam and Elisa host the popular spiritual podcast *Holy
& Human*, hailed as being both sacred and relatable. Known
for making esoteric topics practical and accessible, they help
modern-day mystics remember and reunite with the all-loving,
always-present, wise source of their being. Adam and Elisa offer
client sessions and spiritual retreats, and they host an online mystery school. Learn more at holyandhuman.com.